"A Black Man

My Point of View"

Overcome Male/Female Relationship Drama In The African-American Community

Lawrence R. Mathews J.D., B.B.A.
(Anpu Waset)

11435 West Buckeye Road, #104-202
Avondale, AZ 85323
623-643-9048
lawrencermathews@msn.com
www.lawrencemathews.com

Published by LAWRENCE R. MATHEWS

Book Cover Design by Demetrice Graham.
Book Cover Photos Provided by Anthony Bottoms.

The author is available for lectures and may be reached at the address above.

ISBN 0-9786346-1-6

"Do Not Allow What You Think,
Or The Way You Think To
<u>Limit</u>
What You Think,
Or The Way You Think!"

Anpu Waset

Table of Contents

Introduction.. 1

The Goal of this Book...11

How to Read the Book...15

A Bit about Me...19

SECTION ONE
For the Sisters about the Brothers

Chapter 1
What Do Black Men Want?
What Do Black Men Need? 27

Chapter 2
What Black Men Don't Tell You...........................35

Chapter 3
Genesis of the Two Main Impressions Driving
Black Men...47

Chapter 4
What Does This Have To Do With Me?.....................61

SECTION TWO
For the Brothers about the Sisters

Chapter 5
Genesis of the Main Impressions Driving
Black Women..69

Chapter 6
Brothers, We Don't Get It..............................81

SECTION THREE
Doing the Same Thing Over and Over Again and Expecting a Different Result is a Form of Insanity.

Chapter 7
The Current "Practice" of Relationships is a
Recipe for Disaster...89

Chapter 8
A Typical Impression-Led Relationship...................99

Chapter 9
A Better Way...107

SECTION FOUR
Bringing It All Home

Chapter 10
The Best Way to Use This Book...........................119

Chapter 11
Solutions...125

Chapter 12
Conclusion...139

Chapter 13
Questions & Answers.......................................141

Dedication

This book is dedicated to every woman who longs to meet and be in a relationship with the *right* man. It is also dedicated to every man who longs to meet and be in a relationship with the *right* woman.

Introduction

Greetings!

I am Lawrence R. Mathews. My African name is Anpu Waset. It has many meanings, one of which is "Opener of The Way." I believe that this book "Opens the Way" for African-American people to improve our male- female relationships.

I have written this book specifically for Black Women of African descent in their personal relationships with us, Black Men. However, it is also written for my brethren. There is much contained within these pages that will help our "sisters" to better deal with "brothers" in relationships. There is also much within this book that will help "brothers" better manage relationships with you, our "sisters." The book is a tool to foster discussion among couples about the inner dynamics at play in the relationship setting. One dynamic that many are not fully aware is, simply put, "why" we do what we do in relationships. Not understanding the "whys" or misunderstanding them leads to many of the problems that weigh down the African-American male-female couple in a relationship.

There are plenty of books and talk shows that discuss "what" is done by Black men or Black women to negatively impact their relationships. But few books actually consider "why" in an easy to read, concise manner. I believe that once we understand the "whys," we will be better poised to do what's necessary to improve our relationships. This book will foster a discussion about the "why"—and I believe it will make it easier to do the one thing we all agree is necessary to achieve a positive relationship:

COMMUNICATE!

Communication is something that every couple wants but sometimes has problems doing in relationships.

So often we hear about the need to communicate to improve our relationships. We are told that the inability to communicate will doom a relationship to failure. However, how many people are aware of what *causes* the communication gap in the first place? Wouldn't this be useful information to know?

This book is about one of the underlying causes of the communication gap: *unconscious* **impressions.** An **impression** is the "feeling" one gets as a result of an experience. Getting hit by a car is an experience. Your "feeling" about cars—not wanting to ride in them, not wanting to drive fast, and so on—is the **impression** left behind from the experience. Unconscious **impressions** are the drivers of a person's personality. It is these **impressions** (feelings) which I believe are a major *cause* of the communication gap. They also lead to a host of other problems in our relationships. It is these *"unconscious* **impressions***"* that will be uncovered in this book: **impressions** that form the basis of "why" males and females have problems communicating. ***Impressions*** are also the reason that at the conclusion of the "courting phase," positive and fulfilling relationships seem to be the exception rather than the rule.

Have you ever used the term, *"the exception rather than the rule"?* In the world of African-American male-female relationships, it has been my experience that both men and women want "exception" type relationships rather than "rule" types. Unfortunately I think you would agree that exceptional relationships are few and far between. I have found that both men and women want relationships to improve. However, our ways of achieving improvement is vastly different. We as Black men expect to be afforded a certain level of manhood respect from you our mates prior to taking action to improve a relationship. This manhood respect manifests as a *"feeling"*. I will explain this *"feeling"* in detail in later chapters. Until we get this respect, we are often blind to the concrete problems that occur within the relationship.

From the Black women's perspective, you have ample reason to look at us with disdain. We haven't collectively handled our business well, and we haven't fully supported you as women. We have not yet learned how to communicate our feelings to you. Improvement of the relationship from the female perspective has to be difficult in an environment like this. Although as a group Black women tend to be very good at problem solving and handling their business, without communication, the means to improve relationships just gives you one more thing to do.

What we as Black males and females do not realize is what is "driving" our specific perspective. Hence, the name of the book "A Black Man, My Point of View." My view is that unconscious *impressions* are driving each specific perspective. These *unconscious impressions* cause people to do what they do in relationships. Unconscious *impressions* are also a cause of the communication gap. After reading this book, both you and your mate will have a stronger understanding of the driving force behind both of your personalities.

A word of caution: unconscious *impressions* are often deeply rooted in actions that occurred a long time ago. These actions will be discussed in great detail throughout the book. You may not agree with the premise that past-based actions are the root cause of modern day *impressions.* In fact, you may totally disagree and be emotionally impacted by what is said. This book aims to create a foundation that will allow Black men and Black women to "see" their relationships through their mates' eyes. When we both learn how to "see" from each other's perspectives, then our ability to communicate will grow tremendously. As our ability to communicate grows, so will our ability to foster positive and fulfilling relationships with our mates.

This book is a sincere desire to create a way to foster successful relationships. Although the book is geared to sisters, it is also a book for couples to read together. Brothers will benefit greatly by the words expressed. Finding a husband/fiancé/boyfriend is not hard. Finding a wife/fiancé/girlfriend is not hard. Marrying someone is not hard. Having a COMPLETE AND FULFILLING RELATIONSHIP is HARD! This book will show what Black men think, what drives us, and how that affects Black women. It will also show the *cause* of our inabilities to communicate and lessen the level of frustration in the relationship.

We all know to some extent about how the relationship dynamic works. Women meet us, we meet you. The infatuation stage lasts for one or two years. No one can do anything wrong in this stage. Women "see" us as knights in shining armor. We "see" you as our damsels in distress. We do things for you. Take you out. Show you a good time. You have fun! You "feel" like we are "The Man." We feel like "The Man" with you. Then something happens. Our feelings change. We seem to stop respecting each other. We don't consciously know why but it happens. As men, we may become indecisive, hesitant, and may withdraw. We may even start talking to you less (which was not much in the first place). As women, you may start "discussing" your frustrations with your girlfriend. You may start feeling you are all alone in the relationship. You may start to feel so bad that you begin saying, "I can do bad all by myself!" Before you know it, we are both unhappy in the relationship and don't know specifically why. You may start spending large blocks of time talking to your girlfriends about how disappointed you are with us. We may begin to miss the feelings we had when we first met you.

Black men and women have seen this before. For many of us, it has happened on more than one occasion. Unfortunately, knowing about this dynamic does not help prevent it from happening again. Some people believe that the problem lies with their mate. They seek to find another person (the *right* person) and think things will be better. You can see how this creates a never ending cyclical pattern that ends in frustration. Both men and women are quick to change partners but slow to change the way of thinking about partners.

This book lets you know **why** this scenario plays itself out. I deeply believe that the more Black women understand Black men, the more you will understand yourselves. The opposite is also true: the more Black men understand Black women, the more we will understand ourselves. As we both see how our actions can push certain "buttons" in our mate, we both will be better able to see where these actions originate. Finding this source allows us to deal with *actual* issues as opposed to what *appears* to be an issue.

It has been my experience in relationships that both men and women often respond to "surface" issues instead of the underlying root cause. For example, a sister may seek the advice of her father instead of her husband when forced to make a decision. On the "surface" her mate may think she is just a "Daddy's girl" and spoiled.

However, at the source may reside her sense of "security" with her father that she has yet to feel from her mate. Reacting to the surface "Daddy's girl" issue does not help the situation. It makes it worse. This outer manifestation is not the real problem; the source is—her lack of feeling secure is with her mate. So understanding the source is very important if positive relationships are the goal. This understanding on both levels is important in being able to implement the solutions given at the end of the book.

We've Got the Power!

Black men and women individually exude much strength and power. "Sisters" exhibit an enormous amount of power through how you "handle your business". Also, as first care givers and mothers you are the first shapers of the minds of future generations. This is important to note because many scientists agree that all living human beings originated from a Black woman named Eve in and around Ethiopia in Africa. Black women are the mothers of civilization as we know it. [1]

Black men too have enormous power. We do great things in the sports and entertainment fields, dominating the sports in which we participate. The same is true of the entertainment fields. Russell Simmons and Sean Combs, as the modern day Berry Gordy's, have shown that we can also master the business side of the industry. Please

---

[1] This Eve was one of many other African women. African men existed as well. It is people other than African that come from the loins of Africa.

note that sports and entertainment have a more level playing field for Black men than that of mainstream society, and we thrive when given an equal opportunity. Although we have also made major contributions in the areas of science, math, engineering etc., (Chiek Ante Diop, George Washington Carver, Ernest E. Just, to name a few) accomplishments in these areas have occurred less frequently because the playing field is not level.

Unfortunately for both Black men and women, power is held individually and is rarely brought together in a unified way. Collective power that what you as "sisters" are calling out for today: an unanswered "call" that has made many of you frustrated and often downright angry with us "brothers". I admit that as a group, we have yet to step up completely to the plate and assert ourselves as "men" in society and in our relationships with you. However, our failure to answer the "call" has not been a conscious one. We have not responded because we have consciously chosen not to. We have not responded because we have not yet figured out how to move beyond the effect of the negative *impressions* that drive our decision making—*Impressions* that we do not realize are present.

This book will address those *unconscious impressions*. *Impressions* drive Black male and female actions in intimate relationships. *Impressions* *cause* relationships to need improving in the first place. *Impressions*, when unmasked, allow each of us to "see" from our mate's perspective, opening the communication lines and leading a couple towards harnessing the potential collective power inherent in every relationship. I believe in my heart that when we as Black couples harness this power in a unified way, Pyramids, Sphinxes, and Great Temples for this day and time will be built, structures that will have people thousands of years from today wondering how we built them.

The Goal of this Book

According to *Divorce Magazine,* as a percentage of marriages, the divorce rate in the United States is 49% for all first time marriages. According to *Psychology Today,* 60% of all second time marriages end the same way. These statistics are for all of society. In the Black community it is worse. For example:

▶ The University of Illinois tracked 199 Black and 174 White couples during their first years of marriage. The study found that after three years, 17% of the Black couples were divorced or separated, three times the White percentage.

▶ Analysis of a national survey of 13,017 adults by sociologists Mark Rank and Larry Davis at Washington University in St. Louis found that married Blacks more so than Whites believed that divorce would improve their finances, career, social life, sex life and parenting.

This book will give you a tool that will help your relationship grow in a positive way. The best tool is having an understanding of how men in relationships think. We think *"differently"* from sisters. I know women need to "understand" us, especially in a relationship. This book gives an overview of what Black men want based on our unconscious ***impressions***. The book will show how a man's rearing from boyhood to manhood contributes to his present way of thinking—thinking that is often very different from yours.

I will also show my brethren how sisters have developed their "way of being" with us. We want you sisters to think "differently" than you do about us. It is important for us to be very clear about the unconscious *impressions* that have caused you to respond to us the way you do.

The Chapters in Section 1 are geared to the **sisters** and give an analysis of the unconscious *"impressions"* of Black men and how these manifest in a relationship as wants and needs.

The Chapters in Section 2 are geared to the **brothers** and present an analysis of the unconscious *"impressions"* of Black women and how these manifest as their wants and needs in the relationship.

The Chapters in Section 3 provide an objective look at why we need to change our "way of being" in relationships with an example of how.

The Chapters in Section 4 are the summary, solutions and conclusion of the book. This Section also contains questions and answers.

All of this information is presented so that couples can begin the process of harnessing and unifying the collective power that we have when meaningful relationships are cultivated and nurtured—a process that in far too many cases is the "exception rather than the rule".

“A Black Man, My Point of View”

How To Read The Book

You will get the most out of reading this book OBJECTIVELY! *Read from the perspective of the other party. Men should read the book through the eyes of a woman, and women should read the book through the eyes of a man!* This will allow the material to be absorbed at deeper levels of your being. It will also help to stop the ego from getting defensive when certain portions of the book strike a nerve. You will not learn anything if you are being defensive. This is a book about improving relationships. Therefore, you need to be open in thought and deed as the material is read and absorbed.

This book has been written in four Sections:

Section 1 identifies the wants and needs of Black men and most importantly discusses the genesis of where both originate.

Section 2 does the same for Black women. This section also contains a chapter from me that is a call to the brothers based upon what has transpired to African-American women over the last four hundred years in this country.

Section 3 critically looks at the current model of how people "practice" relationships in this society, a "practice" that is a recipe for disaster! This Section also

"A Black Man, My Point of View"

provides a "new way" of "practicing" relationships—helpful for those who are tired of doing the same thing over and over again in relationships yet expecting a different result.

Section 4 brings everything together and contains solutions to the typical relationship drama and contains specific questions and answers asked by women about Black men in general.

WARNING!!!!!!!!!!!!!!!!!!!!

The first two Sections may provoke a variety of deep emotional responses. These responses may make you not want to read any further. **DO NOT STOP READING UNTIL THE BOOK IS FINISHED!**

The first two sections are foundational and are necessary to "fully" recognize the current state of relationships that are presented in Section 3, and the solutions presented in Section 4. There will be those who will become upset by what is revealed. These sections go to the root cause of where relationship drama begins. Getting to the root of anything takes its toll. (Try getting to the root of a dandelion in your yard.) Some roots are long and are buried deep. Once found, pulling them out is difficult and takes much energy. It is sometimes a wonder how a weed so small above ground (on the outside) can be so long and deep below ground. (on the inside) *Unconscious* **impressions** have long roots and are buried deep. However, there is light at the end of the tunnel. Once roots are understood, dealing with them can be done in a most effective manner.

A Bit About Me

I was motivated to write this book because I was asked by female friends for relationship advice. They told me that my advice was helpful. In essence, they asked me, "Why do men do what they do?" and "What am I doing that may be contributing towards our relationship drama?" These women wanted to better understand men. I know very well about a woman wanting desperately to "understand" her man. I know this because I was married for approximately ten years to a woman who wanted this "understanding" from the beginning to the end of our relationship.

During the entire time of my marriage my ex-wife consistently stated that she wanted to "understand" me. In good times and bad, she stated this consistently. Most of the time I had no clue what it was that she could not "understand." Things seemed very simple to me. Yet for her there was much about me that she could not figure out. We divorced after ten years and I think she "understood" me less at the end of the relationship than she did at the beginning.

Giving the advice spoken of previously made me reflect on the time in my marriage. It also made me realize that other couples (and the women within those couples) were probably experiencing the same thing—

wanting to "understand" their Black Man. That's why I wrote this book.

I am 44 years old, born and raised in Detroit, Michigan. Like many other brothers, my father left my mother when I was about 5 or 6 and my mother never remarried. The neighborhood I grew up in wasn't the best, but the people there did the best they knew how to do. It was poor, but my mother did an excellent job of letting my brother and I feel like we were rich. I had no uncles that I was close to. My grandfather lived in another state. I had no male role models other than the other boys in the neighborhood and the males I saw on television. Unfortunately, I was not the only boy in my neighborhood in this situation.

The "fellas" in the neighborhood had their opinions on what it meant to be a "man" and how women should be treated. The men on television showed roles that differed. The Black men on television then typically were very poor and always out of work or close to being out of work. The men in the movies were pimps and hustlers. There was never a consistent standard. Each boy over time decided for himself what type of "man" he would be.

I made it to college and law school without a positive male role model. The good part was that I made it. The not-so-good part was that I had no clue about what it took to be a "man". I was in college before I learned to do basic things that men do. (Shave and tie a tie for example.) But, these are things men *do*. They do not represent what it means to *be* a man. The bad part was that I had no clue that I had no clue what it meant to be a man. I just thought that because I was 18, I was a man.

There are some of you who may think that a boy with a positive male role model will have a better understanding of what it means to be a man as he grows into adulthood. To a certain extent this is true. However, keep in mind that an environment consisting of mainly negative role models cancels out a great deal of the positivism existing in a household where there is a positive male role model. One bad apple can spoil the whole bunch. Boys growing up in a household with positive male role models will still be constantly pressured by the negative images prevalent in our community. For example a boy growing up with a positive male role model, (his father) who never cheated on his mother, who worked everyday and was a model citizen, will still be pressured by his peer group to act in accordance with the street definition of manhood—a definition centered around sexual prowess. Not wanting to be perceived as being a punk by his "boys/friends", he may strongly feel the pressure to cheat on his girlfriend. This boy will need a great deal of willpower to be like his father and not like his friends. In the end he will probably succeed, but not without a great deal of struggle.

For those of us who grew up without a positive male role model, we strive to be that which we wish we had. This is actually a noble wish. Unfortunately, it leaves a lot to be desired, because it is based on an illusion. It is based on an idea that we had as children of what we "thought" a good father or husband should be. But what does a 6, 7, 8, or 9-year-old child know about being an adult man? I admit that as a child I identified with the concept of fatherhood that I saw on the "Leave It to Beaver" television shows. For me, that image beat the image of James Evans in the television show "Good Times." My preferred image did not work though, as by the time I married; one income was not enough to provide for the household. I mentally held onto the concept of being the provider of the household when the reality was something different. Needless to say this mindset was a contributor to problems that arose in my relationship.

Do not minimize the influence of the neighborhood and societal definitions of manhood. The neighborhood definition differs greatly from that of society at large. As Black boys navigate their way through the neighborhood concept of being a man, we suddenly find that once we become adults there is a new definition—a definition not always easy to live up to in a world not created by us. These differences cause confusion in the psyche of the boy/teen/young man/man. Confusion is what you sisters eventually end up getting from us when we enter into a relationship.

This simplified chronology of my life may seem unimportant right now, but it contributed greatly to me being the type of husband that I was. The chronology of your man's life will help you "understand" him much better. The chronology of Black men's lives will help you "understand" Black men in general.

Sisters, keep in mind the following as you read. First, men think differently from women. To understand us, you must stop wanting us to think like women. One of the main reasons women don't understand men is because women want men to think like women.

Brothers, keep in mind the following as well. Sisters want us to be the men that not only they want us to be but also that "we" want to be. They don't want to nag us. They don't want to pressure us. They are just tired of having to hold it down all of the time and want us to step up to the plate. We too, need to be objective as we look at our mate.

Second, once partners are objective, there is no frustration over the other's "wrong" way of thinking. I find that women in general and "sisters" specifically think they are smarter than us. That may or may not be true. This thinking colors your thoughts about us. To understand us, you must not think from a perspective that you are "smarter than us." The perspective must be that you think "differently from us."

Third, Sisters listen to what **we say** as opposed to what **you want to hear.** Brothers, listen to what our women say and do not dismiss their conversation.

Neither of us needs to allow pre-conceived ideas to prevent either of us from actually hearing what the other has to say.

Fourth, Sisters do not think that your conduct towards us "should" be appreciated by us. I have had more than a few sisters tell me that they have done a lot of things that "should" have made us respond in a particular way. In other words, we should have appreciated your deed. What you fail to recognize is that the man in question may not be "receiving" those things in the way you think we "should." There are many reasons for this. Some of them will be discussed in later chapters of this book. However, our response should not be surprising to you.

SECTION 1

FOR THE "SISTERS"

(About (us) The Brothers)

*"Do Not Allow What You Think,
Or The Way You Think To
<u>Limit</u>
What You Think,
Or The Way You Think!"*

Anpu Waset

Chapter 1

What Do Black Men Want?
What Do Black Men Need?

What do Black men want? What do we need? At the most basic and outer levels we are very simple creatures. We want to please our wives or girlfriends. We want our children to smile when they see us. We want our family to be proud of us. We want peace when we get home from work. We want "a piece" (sex) when we get home from work. We want to watch the game. We want to spend some time with our friends. We want our women to look at us like we are invincible when we have done something big.

On a deeper level we want to be "respected" and we want the "feeling" we get when we are looked up to by our women. We want the "feeling" that derives from pleasing our mates/spouses.

Unfortunately it is my belief that few men are respected or looked up to by women. Consider this:

It appears that there are two camps of thinking among Black women. The first camp wants us (Black men) to be different than we are. This camp does not fully accept us as we are because we should be "different." A difference based upon how this group "thinks" we should be. This group "settles" for us instead of being pleased with us.

The second camp of Black women also "settles" for us but in a different way and from a different perspective. This group feels there is a shortage of Black men, so they have to "settle" for what's out there. They do not like the way we are anymore than those in the first camp. This group accepts us as we are. However, it is done from a place of disgust or contempt.

In both cases it is just a matter of time before sisters begin to outwardly manifest a "feeling" of disrespect for us. This is inescapable, because you never really liked us in the first place. You just didn't consciously realize this when you originally met us. It is difficult to "respect" someone that deep down you really don't like.

Is there another camp that I did not mention? If not, honestly and objectively, Sisters, which camp do you belong to?

First, let's deal with respect. Men want and need to be respected by their women. Black men in society get very little respect.[2] Lack of respect in a relationship is one of the major causes of relationship issues. Black men think you have a "lack of respect" if

---

[2] This will be covered in detail in Chapter 3.

- you do not take a man's last name;
- you do not accept our advice until it is validated by someone else; (generally another man)
- you flaunt the fact that you may make more money;
- you continually bring up every poor decision made;
- you attribute the good decisions to someone else or luck.
- you loudly disagree in public; (This is not an argument but it is being argumentative. This forces us to back down since you won't.)
- you make comments around us but not to us, like "If you want something done, you must do it yourself! Things should get better with two people than worse! I can do bad all by myself!"
- you say that the man is needed only for companionship!
- you let him know that since you make more money than he does, that you are smarter than him.
- you maintaining friendships with other men no matter what he thinks or says.

Respect is an interesting thing. It is not something done overtly or even covertly. Respect is something that is either present or it is not. Nothing has to be said. Nothing has to be done. It expresses as a "way of being." It can be felt.

A woman who respects her man "feels" a certain way about him. You believe in us. You have confidence in us. You know that "we take care of business" or will. This "feeling" makes you proud to take our last name. It makes you want to hear our advice. This "feeling" causes you to eliminate any issue that might jeopardize the relationship. Even when this means discontinuing or altering present relationships.

Respect or this "way of being" expresses as a "feeling." This "feeling" is actually a high level of energy which manifests as pride. I "knew" my family was proud of me when I graduated from Law School. They didn't have to "say" anything. I could "feel" it. Even though I called it a "feeling" or the family being proud of me, energy is actually what I felt. Energy is not static. Therefore the "proud feeling" generated from my family was able to move and be transmitted to me. As energy moves, we "feel" it. This type of energy is positive. Respect is the same kind of energy. A man who "feels" this positive energy from his woman does great things. A woman that does not respect her man also "feels" negative energy. She does not believe in him: she does not have confidence in him; she may have disdain for him in certain ways. This negative "feeling" is also a high level of energy. However, this energy is negative. This negative "feeling" is also felt by us. Over time, this negative energy makes a man indecisive, and he becomes that which you dislike.

His indecisiveness makes for poor decisions. The poorer the decisions, the more negative "feelings" we get from you. Our confidence wanes and as it goes; we look to do less for you as we are reluctant to make another mistake. We become crippled. We become unhappy and seek to again "feel" like a "man." Often to get this positive "feeling" we have an affair with another woman.

All of this happens without a word being spoken by the woman directly to her man. For example, a woman may never tell a man that his idea or suggestion does not make sense. She just doesn't follow it until it is validated by someone she trusts. (Her father, male friends, pastor etc.). The unspoken nature of this communication makes it difficult for anyone to realize it is happening. The woman may not realize that she is knocking him consistently because she never tells him directly and does not recognize her negative "feelings." She calls these negative "feelings" unhappiness, but may not directly attribute this to her man. Resultantly her unspoken negative "feeling" unconsciously grows stronger as the man continues to become the embodiment of that which she does not like.

The man may find another woman from whom he gets the "respect way of feeling" before he formally ends the current relationship. He may not know why he is cheating, because he really does not want to cheat. If men marry, most are ready to be married. Men HAVE to feel respected, to "feel" like men and when it doesn't happen at home we may find it elsewhere.

We also want to be looked up to by our woman. We want to feel like our women trust us. We want to feel like our women believe we can move mountains. When our women believe in us, we believe in ourselves much more and we seek to move mountains. There is nothing that a man would not do for the woman who thinks he can do all things.

Unfortunately, these wants and needs of Black men conflict with Black women's views of relationships and relationship roles.

Harvard sociologist Orlando Patterson has spoken to many black husbands and wives who are disappointed, dissatisfied or disloyal. One overriding problem, according to Patterson, is the issue of sex roles.

> **_"Our men still have male-dominant attitudes towards their spouses but contemporary black women have more independent views about their roles."_**

Men feel like men when they do "manly" things and women do "womanly" things. Like Mr. Patterson stated, women of today don't feel the same way. Black women no longer believe in the traditional roles of previous generations. Their views are independent according to him. This means that there is disagreement about roles that breeds confusion that leads to argument. It does not lead to a man being respected by a woman nor does it allow for a man to "feel" like a man. These views on the roles of men and the women often lead to women making the kinds of statements I mentioned earlier—

statements that are indicative of a subtle unconscious mindset of the woman who does not respect her man. It is this mindset which creates the problem. It is a mindset that many do not recognize or simply choose to ignore and that sometimes leads to a host of problems that are never fully recognized as problems.

The key to fulfilling relationships lies with this recognition. It is the basis of what this book is about and what can be done to overcome it.

What do men want? First, we want to be respected by our woman. Second, we want to "feel" like a man from the woman that we love. Understand this and half of relationship issues from men's perspectives will dissolve quickly.

"A Black Man, My Point of View"

Chapter 2

What Black Men Don't Tell You.

Most Black men were raised by Black women in one form or another. (grandmother, aunt, sister etc.) Most of us grew up wanting to please our mothers. That's why one of the first things that we do when we get the money or ability is to buy them a house or something. We have a need to please our mothers because they raised and taught us. Often they raised us without a father which was not easy. They had to be both our mother and father. We grow up and recognize how difficult this was and look to do something for them. We want to please the person who was the most instrumental in our raising and development. It can be argued that this desire to "please" a woman is a good thing. It is more likely than not that a man who wants to please his mother will also want to please you, his woman. Do you think that a man who has no aspiration to please his mother will want to please any other woman? Sisters tend to belittle Black men's relationships with their mothers. We are called "momma's boys". However, you do not feel the same way about being "daddy's girls". In fact, this is looked at with admiration. Clearly there is a double standard.

Recognize inherent in the desire to please his mom, is the simultaneous desire to please his woman. There is nothing more that a man wants than to be able to please and make you happy, because this is what we want to do. No matter what you may see in our actions and behaviors this is something that we want to do. But this is something that we will not ever tell you.

Often women think that we want to please our mothers more than we want to please you. This is not true. It is actually the opposite, because we want to please you the most. This is not anything we would tell you either because most of us do not consciously realize it. This desire operates at the unconscious level of our being. Deep down, most of us know that our mother's opinions of us are skewed. Therefore, some put little value in what our mothers think about us, because they love us unconditionally.

However, our wife/woman is a much different story. You would not be with us unless you were getting something out of the deal. That something could be love, security, sex or any number of things. But it is not unconditional. [3] Therefore Black men recognize that your love of us is based solely upon us. Mothers' love cannot make us feel like men. In our minds, manhood comes from the feeling transferred to us when our women are pleased by us. This is especially true of Black men like me who grew up without a father. Not only do we want to "please" our wife/woman, we also want to be the father that we didn't have.

---

[3] We do not love you unconditionally either. We want something out of the relationship as well. The inability to love unconditionally is practiced **equally** by both men and women. This inability to love unconditionally is discussed in detail in Chapter 9.

Black men want validation of their manhood from their wife/woman. But again, this is something that we want that you would never know. Unfortunately, this too is an *unconscious* **impression** that most of us do not realize either.

Another aspect that we will never tell you is that we are insecure in large parts of our personality. This is not genetic. In fact it occurs through the school socialization process as a child. In his book, "Countering the Conspiracy to Destroy Black Boys," pg. 28, author Jawanza Kunjufu writes:

> *"Many educators will have us to believe that our boys have low self-esteem; it may be that because they are placed in classrooms where they are slower than the girls (remedial reading), lower-track classes or special education, the schools destroy the boys' self esteem. In all the other endeavors and activities, engaging in sports, listening to rap music, and other social activities, our boys have a high level of self esteem."*

Mr. Kunjufu asserts a difference between what he coins **"school esteem"** and **"self-esteem."** He asserts that what black boys grow up with is a negative **"school-esteem."** They lack the confidence to be successful in a school setting. As a result they do not do as well in school as girls and graduate at lower rates. By itself, this phenomenon could be overcome. Black men who grew up in the 50's and 60's lacked formal education. I assert that they too had a negative *"school-esteem"*. However, they lived during an era when anyone with or without **any** education could work in a factory and bring home middle-class wages. Supporting a family with these types of jobs negated the impact of a negative *"school-esteem"* socialization process. It didn't matter if he could read or write. It didn't matter that he did not excel in the sciences. What mattered was that he had the **opportunity** to provide a comfortable living for his family in spite of his education level or lack thereof.

Today it is a different story. There are few good paying factory jobs that do not require a formal education. In fact, it is almost impossible to find employment without some type of formal education. There are even Black men with doctoral degrees who struggle to find employment commensurate with their level of education and experience. For the man without a high school diploma, or G.E.D., finding a job that will allow him to provide for his family is almost impossible.

In this case *"school-esteem"* quickly turns into negative *"self-esteem"*. Unfortunately, the activities that Black men have high levels of "self-*esteem*" in are in the sports and entertaining fields. There are not enough of those types of jobs to go around.

Couple this trend with the twisted view of "manhood" that Black men embrace and you have substantial room for insecurity to develop in our personalities. According to Michael Brown in *Image of a Man,* the picture of manhood held by most African-American male youth is measured by:

- How much pain or violence can you inflict on another person?
- How many girls can you impregnate without getting married?
- How much reefer can you smoke, pills can you drop, and wine can you drink?
- How many times can you go to jail and come out "un-rehabilitated"?
- How hip are the clothes you wear?
- How much money do you have?
- What kind of car do you drive?[4]

This *image* can be compared with the *image* of manhood described by mainstream White males. Goldberg, in his book *Hazards of Being Male,* writes that a man is:

> "An independent strong achiever who can be counted on to always be in control. His success in the working world is predicated on the repression of self and the display of controlled, deliberate, calculated, manipulative responsiveness. The man who "feels" becomes inefficient because he gets

---

4   Michael Brown, Image of a Man, (New York: East Publications, 1976) pg. 6

emotionally involved and this inevitably slows him down and distracts him. His more dehumanized competition will then surely pass him by."[5]

What do you get when you combine both of these views and limit a man's ability to earn an income to provide for his family? Someone who is a time bomb waiting to explode. And that's what is happening to the men of Black America. We are exploding. It should not be a surprise to see a large number of Black men in jail or engaged in activities which lead to it. It should not come as a surprise to see drug addiction problems in this group. And, it should not surprise anyone to see grown Black men still "rapping" on street corners hoping to get a "record deal." How else are we going to make a good living?

I do not advocate hoping for a "record deal" rather than working the jobs that are available. My aim is to show through these examples what has contributed to an unconscious feeling of *inadequacy* that has developed in Black men. It is difficult to understand the unconscious feeling of *inadequacy* that develops in an environment of perceived hopelessness. Knowing that we cannot compete equally because of factors beyond our control, creates a sort of fear that we cannot provide for our families. Being unable to provide is the ultimate form of failure in a society in which it is instilled that the "man" is the provider of his family. It implies that a man who

---

[5] Herb Goldberg, *Hazards of Being Male,* ,(New York: Signet, 1976), pp. 43-44

cannot take care of his family is not a man. So this sense of *inadequacy* and fear becomes the recognition that the man is actually not a man. Consciously, this is tough to deal with. This is so tough in fact that men often do not deal with it, but instead retreat into drugs, alcohol, and hanging out in the streets. I believe that all men have this sense of *inadequacy,* whether they work or not.

Many men that don't work escape into the streets where there is a defined set of rules for what it means to be a man. (Fighting, making babies etc.). They do not mind the negative connotation that society gives them based upon living this type of lifestyle. They want to "feel" like a man and do NOT want to "feel" inadequate. They do what's necessary to avoid having this feeling.

A Black man who works but provides 50% or less of the family income, has a daunting set of challenges. It is almost impossible for him to avoid having a sense of inadequacy in this setting. He has chosen to live outside of the "street's" definition of manhood. Therefore, he cannot find satisfaction in the street. At home he is doomed to a feeling of inadequacy as he knows that he is not the sole provider for his family. His wife/woman is. In many cases the larger paycheck comes from the wife/woman. Indoctrinated since childhood with the idea that a man is the provider for his family, he knows he is anything but. In this scenario, the development of a sense of inadequacy is inevitable.

Unfortunately many sisters also believe that both of the above ideas constitute what it means to be a man and have co-signed both of these ideals. Some younger women who have identified with the notion of Black males hanging out and rapping, drinking, partying etc., have resigned themselves to believing that it is okay to be with this type of young man. A form of conditioning has occurred. The conditioned feeling becomes that "all" brothers are like this. The younger black woman then "settles" for this type of man. This settling has dangerous consequences, as she now is willing to do an assortment of things to "please" this so-called man. The younger woman now openly takes off her clothes in public for him, thinks it's cute to be called degrading names by him, and even tolerates physical abuse.

The older Black woman ascribes to the idea of the independent strong achiever espoused by Goldberg. A different form of conditioning has occurred in her because she wants an independent strong achiever who can be counted on to always be in control. As long as he takes care of her financially, she accepts his repression of himself. She accepts his inability to communicate, or show his feelings (emotions).

In both instances, a definition of manhood is being practiced and adhered to that we as a race did not define. This definition that has created havoc in our communities. Unfortunately, we do not recognize what is happening at its deepest levels. A perpetual cycle is in effect that breeds generation after generation of Black men that have a deep-rooted sense of *inadequacy*—a feeling that sets Black relationships up to fail before they start. Combine this with the belief that we cannot provide for our families, and you can see that our conduct with you is anything but personal.

It should not be surprising that we would want to "feel" like a "man" and yet never tell you so. This feeling is composed of confidence, pride, strength, mental toughness, physical toughness, respect, and power. Black men want to "feel" like this at all times. However, present-day society was not constructed by Black men for Black men. Therefore, we do not get this "feeling" satisfied in the world. There are two places for us in the world to derive this "feeling." The first is by proving to other men that we are men. This manifests as not being a "punk" and being "hard." These are code words and symbols for wanting to "feel" like a man. Sometimes this macho mentality works when a man proves that he is the toughest among men. However, deep down this is not where we seek validation.

At our core, we seek this validation from our wife/woman. We look within our relationship to get this "feeling" because this is where we actually want to get it. I believe that if we got this "feeling" from our wife/woman, the need for machismo would subside greatly. No matter what others say, the want and need to have this "feeling" from you is one of our drivers (*unconscious **impressions***) in relationships. We as Black men at the deeper core of our being have no other want, need, or desire.

Although we would never tell you about this "feeling", its manifestation occurs in the following ways:

▶ Black men want to know that you, our wife/woman "feels" like you can depend on us.

▶We want to know that you trust our judgment. We understand that any decision that we make may not work precisely. Your decisions will not always work out either. However, we want you to be positive about whatever the circumstances of the decision. We want to "feel" the confidence that you have in us.

▶We want to know that you can learn something from us. It doesn't have to be rocket science or how to do a major experiment. But we want to "feel" like there is something that YOU like in us that we can teach or help you with.

▶We want you to look up to us and "feel" like YOU are really proud to say, "THAT'S MY MAN" without stuttering. We want to "feel" like YOU can gladly say this for at least one reason but preferably more.

▶Last but not least, we "need" to "feel" like YOU need us. The worst "feeling" in the world for a man is the "feeing" that we are not needed by you. This is difficult in the era in which we live. In today's society, many women make just as much money if not more than most of us. Many sisters do not feel you "need" a man to financially "take care" of you. Quite often this is true. This may even be stated to the man in these types of terms, "I don't need you financially," or "I just need you for companionship." This is the ultimate dagger lodged into the heart of a man. We interpret these types of comments as you needing a girlfriend with a penis. From our perspective if this is all you need from us, (companionship) then we are in fact actually not needed.

These are some of the things that Black men would not tell you.

"A Black Man, My Point of View"

Chapter 3

Genesis
Of The Two Main Impressions
Driving Black Men

What are the drivers of the wants and needs of Black men that were discussed in Chapters 1 and 2? Where do they come from and what is their genesis? Are they genetic or are they learned behaviors? And most importantly, can they be overcome?

To fully understand the Black men of today, sisters must be keenly aware of how we were raised. This includes gaining an insight into the physical aspects of our rearing. Were we rich? Were we poor? How many people were in our household? Did we have to do chores? Were we good students? You also need to be aware of the psychological aspects of our rearing, including the environments in which we grew up. These environments include, but are not limited to, the norms of our childhood neighborhoods, the unspoken way of being in our household, the type of television programming we watched. We are a reflection of that upbringing. Ignore these at your peril. Understand these, and you have found a key to making a positive change in your relationship. This knowledge is a tool, for you to initiate "positive actions" from us that will move the relationship forward in a powerful way—a way that stops your relationship from becoming a negative statistic.

To begin this process of understanding us, you will need to first evaluate and reflect upon how we were reared as children by asking:

- What were the environmental factors in place as we grew up?
- Who were our role models? Did we have any?
- What was our household composition? Were Dad and Mom both around?
- Who worked? Who did not? Why Not?
- What was the mood of the neighborhood, City, State & Country?

To understand what makes us tick, (what makes every person tick for that matter) you must recognize that we are the sum total of all of our parts. This means that what you see from us today is a reflection of the sum total of all of our experiences from childhood to adulthood. These experiences created *impressions,* and it is these *impressions* that are important to understand.

To understand "why" we have the wants and needs I've mentioned, you need to recognize that we are the sum total of all these *impressions*. This total makes us the Black men we are today. Many say a person is "the sum total of their experiences". This statement does not go far enough. A person is actually the sum total of the *impressions* they receive from these experiences. People often learn from their previous experiences, however, this knowledge tells people what to do or not do if the same experience happens again. In the span of a person's life, the same type of experience does not always happen. However, the *impression* from every experience stays with a person and affects **EVERY ASPECT OF THEIR LIFE!** It is these *impressions* that actually drive the man (and every person) in ways we don't realize.

Let me give you a brief example. A three-year-old child may see a person on a motorcycle fall off and injure themselves badly. The child gets a "sick feeling" seeing the person injured in this way. As the child grows up, he/she will forget seeing the fall because of his/her age. However, every time he sees someone on a motorcycle he/she may get the same "sick feeling." A feeling now that he/she cannot explain. This "sick feeling" may keep him from riding a motorcycle. It may cause him to get upset when a loved one rides a motorcycle. It could cause an argument in his household if someone wanted to get a motorcycle. This "sick feeling" (*impression*) drives all of these actions and reactions and often cannot be explained. Although the experience of the motorcycle accident has long gone and been forgotten, the unconscious *impression* of that experience is still directing aspects of his/her life. Remember:

Impressions **stay with people for life!**
Depending upon the *impression*, they can also unknowingly be passed from one generation to the next!

The good news is *impressions* can be removed. However, this process requires time and effort and first a thorough understanding of their existence.

To fully understand Black men, you must fully understand the *impressions* that drive us. Some of the *impressions* can be attributed to our direct experiences as children and/or youth. With careful thought and consideration, *impressions* derived from previous experiences can be discovered. Once you discover some of the experiences which have occurred, you can gauge the type of *impression* that was left by them. *Impressions* from direct experiences are not that difficult to uncover while other *impressions* are not as easy.

Some *impressions* are passed down through generations. These *impressions* are formed without a direct experience. Family codes or values rarely verbally spoken are easily understood by all within a family. They are unwritten but everyone knows them and is moved by them. These codes or values can pass through 4 or 5 generations and also leave lasting *impressions* that can be almost impossible to find—unless you know where to look.

To gain an insight into the overt (outward) *impressions* that drive your man, become a good listener, especially when we talk about our childhood or youth. On this subject, we openly share our experiences with whoever will listen. Concentrate on our body movements as we talk about these experiences. We become animated and more verbal about experiences that made a lasting impact. Ask us how we felt as a result of the experience, and whether we have had the same experience more than once. Find out about the pleasurable as well as the unpleasurable experiences. An *impression* was made from each one and the sum of all of these unconscious *impressions* now drives us.

For example, as children we may have had a mother who did not give open displays of affection when we fell and physically hurt ourselves. This may have been contrary to what we saw the other mothers doing with our friends. The *impression* left from this experience could be that we feel we are not deserving of affection when hurt. As an adult, we may seem odd to you when we shy away from physical displays of affection. You want to be there for us, but for "some reason" we will not allow you to be. When you ask us "Why?", we close up and shut down. Although we may want to, we are at a loss to explain this "uncomfortable feeling."

Without an explanation many negative things can happen. You may think that the problem is you. You may start to think negatively about yourself. You may question us further for answers, but because the *impressions* are unconscious, we are not able to answer. We then grow frustrated with your continued asking of the same questions over and over again. We consider this to be nagging. This frustration builds and erupts. It can lead to arguments over little things such as the cap being left off the toothpaste. Anything can set either person off. All of this can happen, and it happens quite often because people are not aware of this "unexplainable uncomfortable feeling."

Fortunately, the ***impression*** derived from a direct experience can be determined. The ***impressions*** derived from an indirect one are much more difficult to discover.

Indirect ***impressions*** in many instances drive the personality much more than those gained from direct experiences. I'd like to talk about two of the main ***indirect impressions*** that drive us.

A major indirect ***impression*** driving the Black man is the "feeling" that he cannot support his family. Jawanza Kunjufu in his book, *Countering the Conspiracy to Destroy Black Boys,* (pg 131) stated:

> "African American men, like European men, are taught to be aggressive, to not cry, show little emotion and affection toward male children, to ignore symptoms of ill health, and to continue to bring home the bacon. African American men though, have a difficult time bringing home the bacon, in contrast to their European counterparts. African American adult male unemployment hovers at 25%, and teenage unemployment is soaring to 75%, with a strong possibility that some will *never* work. Imagine what it

is like in a male-controlled world to not be able to bring home the bacon. Is there any worse conspiracy than miseducation of African American boys so they will never compete in the economy?

Elliot Liebow, in *Talley's Corner,* (pgs 210-213) says:

"The way in which the man makes a living and the kind of living he makes have important consequences for how the man sees himself and is seen by others; and these in turn, importantly shape his relationships with family members, lovers, friends and neighbors.

Making a living takes on an overriding importance at marriage. Although he wants to get married, he hedges his commitment from the very beginning because he is afraid not of marriage itself, but of his own ability to carry out his responsibilities as a husband and father. His own father failed and had to "cut out" and the men he knows who have been or are married have also failed or are in the process of doing so. He has no evidence that he will not. The black menial worker remains a menial worker so that, after one, two or three years of marriage and many children, the man could not support his family from the very beginning and is even less able to support it as time goes on.

The longer he works, the longer he is unable to live on what he makes. He has little vested interest in such a job and learns to treat it with the same contempt held for it by the employer and society at large. From his point of view, the job is expendable; from the employer's point of view, he is. Sometimes he sits down and cries at the humiliation of it all. Sometimes he strikes out at her or the children with his fists, perhaps to lay hollow claim to being man of the house in the one way left open to him, or perhaps simply to inflict pain on this woman who bears witness to his failure as a husband and father and therefore as a man.

Increasingly, he turns to the street corner where a shadow system of values constructed out of public fictions serves to accommodate just such men as he, permitting them to be men once again provided they do not look too closely at one another's credentials. [6]

These writers accurately describe the mindset of most Black men, and the "feeling" that we are not men

---

[6] Elliot Liebow, *Tally's Corner,* (Boston: Little, Brown, 1967), pp.210-213.

because we are not able to provide financially for our families. This "feeling" is the *impression—an impression* that drives us every time money or support is mentioned in the household, whether married or not.

This *impression* has very long roots. This *impression* started during the days of slavery. Dr. Na'im Akbar in his book, *Chains & Images of Psychological Slavery,* (pg. 28) said the following about the definition of "manhood" for the enslaved African:

> "The African-American man was evaluated by his ability to endure strenuous work and to produce children. He was viewed by the slave master as a stud and a work horse. The stronger and more children he could sire, the greater the expansion of the master's slave holdings and the greater was his financial worth. The more work the slave could perform, the greater the production, and the greater were the profits that came to the master. African-American manhood was defined by his *ability to impregnate a woman and the degree of his physical strength.*
>
> The virtues of being able to protect, support and provide for ones offspring, which is the cornerstone of true fatherhood, was not considered the mark of a man. In fact, the slave who sought to assert such rights for

his offspring was likely to be branded as a trouble maker and either punished or killed. After several generations of such unnatural treatment, the African-American man adapted and began to avoid the role of a true father.

Today in African-American communities around America, we carry the mark of the strong-armed stud from slavery. He occurs as the modern-day pimp or the man who delights in leaving neglected babies dispersed around town. He is the man who feels that he is a man only by his physical, violent or sexual exploits. He leaves welfare (***modern day master***) or chance to father his children—and he fathers his "ride."

Emphasis and (words) added.

Unfortunately for Black men, the negative *impression* of "feeling" like we cannot provide for our families occurs in ways more than financial. It also occurs mentally through a "feeling" of "personal inferiority" which is the second major indirect *impression*.

The affects of the institution of slavery on our ancestors and us as their descendants has been chronicled extensively by many authors. Some say that the effects of slavery leave no lasting impact. Others disagree. There are many views on the subject, and I will not debate the pros or cons of either position. Personally, I do believe though that the institution of slavery left a lasting *impression* on everyone associated with the practice. The present descendants of the slaves deal with the *impressions* left by this travesty. The country as a whole does so as well. The *impressions* formed over one hundred years ago drive significant aspects of people's personalities today.

Dr. Na'im Akbar on page 20 of the same book said the following regarding the "personal inferiority" of the African who had become a slave:

> "The shrewd slave-makers were fully aware that people who still respected themselves as human beings would resist to the death the dehumanizing process of slavery. Therefore, a systematic process of creating a sense of inferiority in the proud African was necessary in order to maintain them as slaves. This was done by humiliating and dehumanizing acts such as public beatings, parading them on slave blocks unclothed, and inspecting them as though they were cattle or horses. Young children were separated from their mothers because the mother's love might cultivate some self-respect in the child.

The slaves were kept filthy and the very nature of physical restraints over long periods of time began to develop in the people a sense of their helplessness. The loss of the ability to even clean one's body and to shield oneself from a blow began to teach the slave that he should have no self-respect.

These things, combined with the insults, the loss of cultural traditions, rituals, family life, religion, and even names, served to cement the loss of self-respect. With all kinds of images of Africans as dirty and only half human, it was inevitable that a sense of inferiority would grow into the African-American personality.

Sisters, suffice it to say that there are two **indirect impressions** that you should be aware of when dealing with us. Those **impressions** are the *"feeling of personal inferiority"* and the same *"feeling" made worse by living in a society where the opportunity for Black men to support their families is limited*. These **impressions** create an overall "feeling" of "inadequacy." We do not describe this as inadequacy because consciously we do not recognize that it is there. For us it is just a "feeling" which we do not tell you exists. These are our two biggest unconscious **impressions** which drive our personality. It is these drivers which cause our inability to communicate. Hence the communication gap. Drivers which are difficult if not impossible to discuss since for many of us we do not realize they are there.

Chapter 4

What Does This Have
To Do With Me?

Ultimately this is the question for sisters. What does an understanding of Black's men's wants, needs and desires have to do with you? Should it matter that you are aware of the things we do not tell you in our relationships? Does it make any difference whether you are aware of the impressions that drive our personality? Better yet what's in it for you?

It is very important to FULLY understand what makes us tick. For too long we as a race have handled our relationships from the perspective of being reactionary. This means that we go into relationships "responding" to what appears to be happening as opposed to "initiating" actions in accordance with a mindset that will prevent specific reactions from happening.

For example if you have a baby, and the infant learns that when it cries it will get some type of attention, (a hug, feeding, a diaper change, whatever) the child will begin to do this automatically when any of these needs arise. You as the child's parent at first will "respond" (react) to the cry. Since you do not know what is "driving" the crying, you do all of these actions for the baby until you figure out which one is needed. You give the baby the bottle, but the baby cries anyway. You check the baby's diaper, but it is not wet. You check the baby's sleeping area and lo and behold you find that baby has rolled over on its pacifier and is uncomfortable. You remove it and baby feels better and stops crying.

Over time you become much clearer in recognizing that since baby cannot communicate, it is better for you and baby to not wait to "respond" to baby's needs. You then become pro-active. You check baby's diaper regularly. You feed baby regularly. You inspect baby's play area regularly. You "initiate" actions before you have something to "respond" (react) to. This pro-action does not prevent baby's cries completely; however, it does eliminate much of it. Additionally, it gives you one less thing to think about when you actually "respond" to baby's cries.

What does this have to do with a relationship with Black men? A great deal. Many Black women are very accustomed to being responsible for a lot of things. You work and make good money, raise children, and do everything necessary to make your household run in an efficient manner—all of this, many times without the aide of a husband/man. Sisters, as a group, are the most responsible people I know. You have grown to be responsible "fix it" types of people. In the case of the baby, you "fix" baby's cries by "finding" a solution. (you react)

However it seems you have grown tired of being responsible. You have a desire to have a husband/ man.

You desire a strong Black man who can be responsible while you lean on him. Based on this desire, once you find what "appears" to be a strong Black man, you do what you think is necessary to make the relationship work. You "respond" to us by trying to "fix" what appear to be problematic areas for us. Unfortunately, your "responses" (reactions) are not typically what we are "crying" out for. In this case "the baby" may need to be changed but you are attempting to feed it. Since your "response" in this case is incorrect, "baby" continues to cry and you "respond" to something else. Typically this next response (reaction) is incorrect also.

Black men are not babies; nor do we want to be treated as such. The point of the example is that in your desire to make the relationship work (fix it), you do things that do not necessarily help. Often you react to things that you perceive to be problems for us. Your goal is to be helpful, but your initiative often does not help. In fact, your reaction sometimes makes things worse. Because you do not understand us and what is driving us, your help becomes everything but that.

This is why an understanding of our wants and needs is important. In the preceding example, the baby's wants and needs were to be fed, changed, and hugged, not necessarily in that order. Knowing the baby's wants and needs allowed mother to be "specific" in her "response" (reaction) as opposed to haphazard. As the level of knowledge about the baby's wants and needs grows, what was once a "response" becomes pro-action.

A shift occurs. Mothers begin to "initiate" actions more and "respond" (react) less.

In the relationship arena, Black women "respond" (react) to what **you** think our wants and needs are. You give us money even if we don't ask. You give us your credit card even when we don't ask. You are there at our beck and call. You "respond" (react) quickly to every cry for the sake of having the relationship you have always wanted. All of these responses/reactions require much work and energy. Therefore, you are working very hard for the betterment of the relationship RIGHT NOW! Unfortunately, what you are doing presently does not address our wants and needs. It does the exact opposite. It feeds a negative aspect of us that does not need feeding anymore. Your "responses" (reactions) contribute to our current sense of feeling *inadequate.*

In spite of you doing all these things to make the relationship work, we still leave, or cheat, or do not commit fully. Somewhere in the relationship your actions, that you think are so wonderful, are actually "feeding" our sense of *inadequacy.* Recognize that you do not <u>create</u> the sense of *inadequacy.* It was present before we met you. However, often this sense is worsened by the type of help that you voluntarily give. Giving that you perceive as unconditional and wonderful.

Understanding what makes us tick will allow you to "re-direct" the actions that you are already presently engaged in, (that do not work) into actions that will address us at our core. This will **not** give you more work to do. Understanding us will allow you to give quality to the actions that you are already doing. Now with this perspective you will be able to initiate actions that will mean something to us.

In the example with the baby, were the mother's actions with the baby done for the mother or for the baby? They were for the baby. Therefore your actions with us in a relationship also should be done for us. **Not for you!**

Do not give us your credit card because **you** think that is what a good woman should do. This is an action that YOU think is appropriate. We need to "feel" like men. A kind word, encouragement or belief that we will succeed goes much further than the credit card. **You** think the credit card helps. However, in this case **you** are not the issue. The issue is what is best for **us.**

What action by you towards us will give us a sense of empowerment? A sense of strength? What actions can you do which could help negate the inner sense of *inadequacy* that many of us have? This is the key. Do not do things for us that you think we should like. Do things that will address the fundamental core of our being. This will not require you to do anything more than you already do. It will require you to re-direct your present way of "being" with us. We will positively respond to that. At that point you won't have to wonder why we are not the men you want. You will begin to see us transform into the men we are capable of being right before your eyes.

SECTION 2

FOR THE "BROTHERS"

(About the Sisters)

*"Do Not Allow What You Think,
Or The Way You Think To
<u>Limit</u>
What You Think,
Or The Way You Think!"*

Anpu Waset

Chapter 5

Genesis of the Main *Impressions* That Drive Black Women

Prior to the last two chapters, the discussion centered on the aspects of Black men's personalities that makes us "tick." However, relationships do not occur in a vacuum. Sisters bring their own set of experiences and unconscious *impressions* into the relationships that color their view of us. What are these experiences? What unconscious *impressions* have you been left with as a result? How do these *impressions* manifest themselves in the relationship? What happens when your actions colored by previous *impressions* come face to face with our actions also colored by previous *impressions?* Do they ever co-exist in an amicable fashion that produces a complete and fulfilling relationship?

Before discussing specific *impressions* that I believe drive Sisters, (*impressions* that butt heads with ours in the midst of the relationship) let me remind you of the difference between an experience and an *impression*. An experience is the act itself. Being hit by a car is an experience. Your "feeling" about cars, not wanting to ride in them, not wanting to drive fast, and others, is the *impression* left behind from the experience. Experiences are intermittent. *Impressions* from those experiences may last a lifetime. They also can be passed from one generation to the next.

We now focus on three specific *impressions* that I believe beset the African-American woman. There are more, but I will address three:

The first is the mistaken *idea* that she has to be strong and independent. This *impression* causes a *"fix it" mentality.* This woman is always trying to "fix" something. She typically fixes things well in most arenas except one—relationships.

The second *impression* is the *idea* that equates love with having many children by different men. What drives this woman is the need to be loved unconditionally. Unfortunately, it's a case of looking for love in all the wrong places.

The third and final *impression* is a women's need for security. In many ways this *impression* is the basis of the first *impression* of being strong and independent. Because of a "feeling" of insecurity from her man or men in general, she overcompensates and creates a shield of strength and independence. This woman then flexes this strength and independence to the man she wants to receive security from but doesn't.

All of these *impressions* are brought to the relationship and interact with the *impressions* that we men bring to it. When all of them are brought together, the result is not pretty.

I believe that there are two different types of Black women today. The first is the strong independent type who brings home "the bacon," fries it up in a pan and "takes care of her business". Then there is the woman who is content to have many children by many fathers and is never completely able to take care of herself or her children. Both types often exhibit the most unfortunate condition of believing that they cannot live without a man. Women with this condition will stay with a man even though he is no good for her. These are the two types that I see. Have you ever wondered where either of these mentalities came from? I know I have. Do you think that either mindset is reflective of Black women in general? If true, you would expect to see the same behavior patterns in other women of color in other countries all over the world. But we don't see this anywhere else but here in the USA. Is it possible that both types are learned behaviors?

I take the position that both mentalities are learned behaviors based upon growing up in this part of the world in this particular society. These behaviors occur as a result of *impressions* from the collective community experience and from personal experiences.

One of the places where similar experiences are shared by women of African-American descent is in the home where girls are reared. Girls are raised very differently than boys.

The ***impressions*** of girls left by these experiences have consequences for them as they grow and become adult women—women who will eventually become involved in relationships with men.

Dr. Jawanza Kunjufu, in his book, *Countering the Conspiracy to Destroy Black Boys,* (pg 128) talked about the difference in child rearing practices for girls and boys. He said the following about its impact on male-female relationships:

> "Men may enter these relationships with fewer academic, economic, emotional and domestic skills. They may expect women to love them unconditionally and to be as loyal to them as their mothers are. Women who saw their mothers do everything without a man will be aggressive and more academically accomplished, as well as emotionally and domestically self-sufficient. A woman would like for her man to demonstrate these same qualities, but because of the way she has been raised, as opposed to the male track record, she often feels that it is in her best interest to keep a little money on the side, just in case."

Have women been raised in a way that differs from that of men? You bet they have. Women (especially those without a husband) raise their daughters to be independent. They raise them to "take care of their business". They know that a man is likely to leave, so they instill within their daughters the need to be able to take care of themselves, without the need of a man. Mothers stress education for girls. They give girls chores that instill discipline, and they demand that they be responsible for themselves.

You often see little Black girls no more than 10-12 years old preparing breakfast for their 7-year-old siblings and walking with them to school after the mother has already left for work. The young girl brings her siblings home from school, makes sure their homework is completed, warms up the food that mom prepared and feeds everyone by the time mom arrives home from work. The girl excels in school. She gets straight A's in the midst of this difficult circumstance. This girl does all of this even though she has a 14-year-old brother who does nothing. He does not help around the house. He does not do his homework. He doesn't listen to much of anything that his mother has to say.

Why do mothers raise their daughters in this way and do something entirely different with their sons?

There may be a historical basis for it. What follows is an excerpt from an article written approximately 300 years ago. A comparison of the content of the excerpt with the mindset and attitudes of Black women in general today will show striking similarities. The excerpt is a part of a speech delivered by a white slave owner named William Lynch on the bank of the James River in 1712. [7] There is much more to the speech than what follows. This excerpt addresses the present issue only.

"THE BREAKING PROCESS OF THE AFRICAN WOMAN"

Understanding is the best thing. Therefore, we shall go deeper into this area of the subject matter concerning what we have produced here in this breaking process of the female nigger. We have reversed the relationships. In her natural uncivilized state she would have a strong dependency on the uncivilized nigger male, and she would have a limited protective tendency toward her independent male offspring and would raise the female offspring to be dependent like her. Nature had provided for this type of balance.

<u>We reversed nature by burning and pulling one civilized nigger apart and bull whipping the other to the point of death—all in her presence.</u> By her being left alone,

---

[7] The Willie Lynch Letter & Making of a Slave, published by Lushena Books, August 1999.

unprotected, with the male image destroyed, the ordeal caused her to move from her psychological dependent state to a <u>frozen independent state.</u> **In this frozen psychological state of independence she will raise her male and female offspring in reversed roles. For fear of the young male's life, she will psychologically train him to be mentally weak and dependent but physically strong.**

Because she has become psychologically independent, she will train her female offspring's to be psychologically independent. *What have you got?* You've got the nigger woman out front and the man behind and scared. This is a perfect situation for sound sleep and economics.

I submit that the difference in the rearing of Black girls and boys occurs based upon ***impressions*** from previous experiences that have been passed down throughout generations. An objective look at the collective experience of the African-American community and its present manifestations does not seem to be coincidental.

As we have seen, Black women on the plantation raised their sons to be psychologically weak and physically strong. They did this *knowingly* for fear of raising a son who would grow up to receive the same type of treatment she saw inflicted on the strong Black man pulled apart or beaten to death in front of her eyes. Black women today still raise their sons to be psychologically weak and physically strong. Today we call this being over-protective. But this is done *unknowingly*. This way of rearing her son is the outward manifestation of generations-old unconscious **impressions** that seek to "protect" him from the world. Black mothers do not know how to raise psychologically strong boys because they have not seen psychologically strong Black men. It is very difficult, if not impossible, to teach something that you do not know or have never seen.

Conversely, Black women on the plantation raised their daughters to be psychologically independent. They did this *knowingly* for reasons of survival. They knew that there was no security for them as their "protection" (man) had been emasculated by the plantation owner. Internally they knew their girls would have to fend for themselves now that their protection, (the black man) was no longer there for them. These mothers knew that their girls would have to be mentally tough to withstand the raping that would soon occur from the slave master and his children. These mothers knew that their girls would have to be mentally tough when forced to mate with male slaves that they did not know or like for the sole purpose of having children that would benefit the slave master's profits. These mothers knew that these girls would probably be sold at a young age and would be totally responsible for themselves. In a short time, these girls would be at the mercy of others who were strangers.

Black women today also raise their daughters to be independent. Even today there is a feeling of insecurity when thinking about Black men. It is my belief that this type of rearing occurs as a result of unconscious *impressions* from the plantations. Today it is also done for survival. However survival today is equated with not being able to depend on a black man.

These are the three major unconscious *impressions* that Black women have that make a happy relationship difficult to achieve. There are other *impressions* as well but these three, feeling <u>insecure, expressing insecurity as independence with no need of a man</u> and <u>seeking love through having many children</u> are the ones that contribute the most towards unhealthy relationships.

Any one of these *impressions* makes a successful relationship difficult to achieve. The independent type of woman is attracted to what she perceives is a strong Black man. However, her perception is just a perception as she does not have a basis for knowing what true strength in a Black Man is. She has never seen it, so what she "sees" as strength is only an idea in her own mind. An idea which is not based in reality. Therefore, it is only a short period of time before she realizes that the man does not embody the strength that she thought was there. Once her perception of strength in him fades, she is left with having to handle her business alone once more. She soon discovers that the strength that she thought was there was just a self-created illusion in her own mind. He is no different than any other brother. Relationship drama soon follows.

The dependent Black woman has many lovers and often has children by many of them. The *impression* driving her is the idea that love is received through sex or from children that will love her unconditionally. This *impression* parallels Black women on the plantation. Living beings have a need to love and be loved. On the plantation this was not possible for the slaves. For the 8 to 13-year-old Black girl being raped by the slave master and his children, forced to mate with other slaves she did not know, and sold from plantation to plantation, finding love was almost impossible. In the midst of this sick type of mental conditioning, a sick mindset developed—a mindset that began to equate love with the sum total of her experience: sex with many different men and having many children. The phenomenon is no different in families where abuse is common and people grow up thinking that abuse is love. It is the same type of mindset. What was/is "driving" this girl of the past and this same girl/woman of today is to be loved unconditionally. The way she finds to be loved unconditionally (sex with many men & many children) does not appear to provide the love that she desires. This unconscious "driver" or "way of thinking" also does not help foster positive relationships.

Positive and successful relationships are few and far between in today's world. Recognition of the possible unconscious *impressions* that may be driving you is important in having the type of relationship that you want. This understanding will help both partners recognize their contribution to negative aspects of their relationships. It will also allow you to see that Black men's negative actions towards "Sisters" in the relationship are not necessarily personal.

Impressions and their manifestations "drive" all people in relationships. Misunderstanding their impact or having no knowledge of their impact makes having a successful relationship almost impossible.

“A Black Man, My Point of View”

Chapter 6

Brothers, We Don't Get It!

For a brief moment I want those who read these words, (especially my Black male brethren) to look at the situation of relationships from the eyes of "Sister's." Look at it OBJECTIVELY. Imagine for a moment being a woman who at one time in her history watched many of the biggest and strongest of Black men, killed in the most barbaric of ways: beaten to death, set afire while alive, physically torn apart by being tied to different horses forced to run in different directions. What impact do you think this would have on you?

The biggest and strongest of men represent the "protector" that women naturally seek in their man. This natural sense of protection was completely destroyed. Could women have anything but a sense of hopelessness after seeing these types of atrocities against what they deemed as their "protectors"? What were they to do when the slave master and his children raped them at the ages of 8 to 13 and beyond? What were they to do when they were forced to mate with other men for the sole purpose of having children for the slave master's holdings? How "*secure*" could they be and most importantly, what could these little girls teach the children born from these types of unions?

It had to be difficult for them at that time in our history. But the times never really changed. Even after slavery had officially ended, Black women were still at the mercy of White men and the White men's children. There are many books and articles that have been written about the folly and play that White men and women found in lynching Black men. The end of slavery did not mean that the Black woman's "protector" was now in a position to "protect" her. Black men were still at the mercy of White males in the United States' so-called Democratic system, so she still had no basis for feeling "*secure*."

Through the 1930s, '40s, and '50s, the practice of lynching gradually subsided. However, Black men did not begin to be the "protectors" of their women. Black men were still being killed by White men for numerous reasons. Some were killed because they were not "good nigga's". Even teenage boys, (Emmit Till) was barbarically killed because of allegedly "looking" at a White woman.

The 1960s, '70s, '80s and '90s saw a shift from the outright killing of Black men to the wholesale incarceration of Black men. The killing by Whites stopped and was replaced by a new method—jailing. A Black male in jail cannot "protect" or provide for a family. At the conclusion of his sentence if convicted of a felony, he still cannot provide for a family as employment opportunities are rare for those with a criminal record. Even today in the 21st century, Black women still do not have a basis for feeling "protected" (*secure*) from us as Black men.

From the days we arrived on the shores of this country against our will through today, Black women have had to fend for themselves, by themselves. With this as a backdrop, it is not difficult to understand why Black women think the way that they do about us. They have a reason to be mad at us. We as Black men allowed another group of men to destroy us and our families.

They have a reason to want to be loved unconditionally, especially by us. Have we as Black men loved our women unconditionally? Has anyone? It should not be surprising to see young women wanting children so they can have someone they think will love them unconditionally.

What about the women who have been married to the same man for 25-50 years? Do they have reason to be upset with their mate and lot in life? It should not be surprising to note that many of these women feel like their life was wasted. Depending on their age, they were not afforded the opportunity to get a college education. Therefore, they are now stuck with a man they may not like because they totally depend upon him. However, even in this situation in which the man "handled" his business and provided for his family, this dependence was not complete. Was this man in fact and in deed her "protector?" Did the fact that he was with her over a 30-50 year time period mean that he was the protector of her? The answer is no. This man was still subject to the spoken and unspoken rules and regulations of society at large. Rules given and dictated by White men. This man was no more a protector of the Black woman than she was, because he did not control his family or his community's way of thinking.

It is my opinion that the conscious creation of societal norms and the way people think about life and how it is to be lived is the true measure of manhood. White males have done a superior job over the last one thousand years of creating societal norms, rituals, and thinking patterns that people have believed to be true or the best. Even when those same norms, rituals and thinking patterns had barbaric and negative consequences on different groups of people. The Black man married for 30-50 years has not done this. Therefore, even his wife of many years may also be upset or disappointed with this man.

Some people object to the way modern young women allow themselves to be used as sex objects for money or other reasons. Isn't this what she was used for on the plantation of the slave master? How could she mentally survive this negative circumstance if she didn't create reasons to justify the treatment perpetuated upon her? This woman had no choice. It was strictly a matter of "survival." Although allowing oneself to be someone's sex object today is not a case of survival in that sense, it is indicative of the same type of mindset—a mindset stemming from unconscious generations-old *impressions* handed down to us from our ancestors that as a people in the 21st century are not aware of.

Brothers, our sisters need two things from us. First, they need a lot of compassion. Walking in their shoes has not been easy. We have been around them yet they have been alone. It is much easier to deal with loneliness while alone, than it is to be alone with someone standing or living right next to you. Second, they need us to step up and be the men that they want us to be, men that our ancestors would be proud of today and unconsciously men that we want to be too.

We must now tackle and resolve the issue that causes so many problems in relationships today. We as a group of people must determine what life is, what it is about, and how it is to be lived. We must develop and then implement a new mindset that we as Africans in America can live our lives by, from this day forward. We must choose what we as a people will think and then create institutions that will reinforce that belief. This is what we must do and this is what we must start doing today!

"A Black Man, My Point of View"

SECTION 3

DOING THE SAME THING OVER AND OVER AGAIN AND EXPECTING A DIFFERENT RESULT IS A FORM OF INSANITY!

“A Black Man, My Point of View”

Chapter 7

The Current Practices in Relationships are RECIPES FOR DISASTER!

At the end of Chapter 6 I indicated that it is time for us as Black men to create a view of life and how it is to be lived and then create institutions that will support that view. Since this is a book about relationships, then this is the first step in creation for us to do. For this to happen most effectively, we must objectively analyze the current view of relationships. The phrase "you don't know, what you don't know" can often be true. Before we consciously determine a new/different way of thinking and being in our relationships, it would be wise to be keenly aware of our present way of thinking and being.

This Chapter discusses in detail the current practices in relationships, practices that are ingrained and accepted by people as normal. However, they are only normal because most people engage in them. If we review them carefully, they are actually abnormal. I call these practices "recipes for disaster!"

What follows is an analysis of male/female relationships and the current view that both males and females have regarding them. This chapter looks critically at the WANTS/NEEDS that people say they have in relationships. You will see that many people have the same wants/needs in relationships. You will see how our present ideas about relationships prevent us from having what we say we want—a fulfilling and long-lasting relationship. Current ideas and practices do the opposite, because they set relationships up to fail.

People think they want relationships.
They don't.
They really want their needs and desires met.

With that as a backdrop, I want to draw your attention to an ***impression*** (not mentioned previously) that is detrimental to having a positive and fulfilling relationship—an ***impression*** that is important to be aware of when creating a new way of thinking and being in a relationship. I believe that people across the color divide, do NOT want relationships! I believe that people actually want their ***idea*** of someone who will fulfill *their* <u>wants</u> and <u>needs</u>. This ***idea*** is ego driven. It is strictly a reflection of what a person can get *from* another person in a relationship. Although people say they want a complete and fulfilling relationship through word, speech and behavior, people's ***actions*** in a relationship provide a better indication of what people really want.

The *idea* that a complete and fulfilling relationship happens when there is someone in your life who provides for your wants and needs is an impression. This idea is an unconscious **impression** that is the driver behind each person's actions within the relationship. This *idea* is something that we must become aware of. A great relationship has nothing to do with love, unless **you** want to get love out of it. A great relationship has nothing to do with fulfillment unless **you** want to get fulfillment out of it.

The present societal view of relationships and its associated mentality that is currently practiced could directly be taken from the song by Janet Jackson. "What have you done for me lately?" This view is evident when an objective analysis is done looking at the reasons that relationships begin and fail.

Do people really want a relationship? Or do they want someone who will provide them with what they have determined they want or need? A relationship is searched for and developed to satisfy an **individual's** specific wants/needs. Relationships are not about love. Nor are they about coming together with your "soul mate." That is what people say through their words. That is not what is real. The reality for a person is having someone you can call your own (ego) who will "give **you** what **you** want, when **you** want it." Objectively speaking, there is nothing loving about it. Unless you consider love a reflection of getting what **you** want when **you** want it, and falling out of love when *you* stop getting what *you* want when *you* want it.

Let's look at some common relationship examples so that you can see for yourself how often this mindset is practiced.

When a person is attracted to another person, what is it that is so attractive about the other person? What are the words spoken to describe this attraction? Men and women both often say things such as "she looks good," or "he's so fine!" Whose perspective are these comments coming from? Your own. So the other person looks good to *you!* What happens next? When you are around this person, don't *you* feel good? Isn't it common to hear people say "he makes *me* feel so good when I'm with him," or "*I* feel like I am on top of the world when I am with her"? Do these comments have anything to do with the person for whom you have developed an infatuation? No. They all are based upon *you and what you are getting from being around this person! YOU* get a "good feeling."

That's the beginning of a potential relationship when you meet someone new. But what happens as the relationship develops? What solidifies the idea that you may be falling in love or may now be in love with this person? The fact that this person fulfills a good portion of *your* wants and needs. For example, a woman who wants security may see this trait in a man who may hug her a lot, or have lots of money or be a big man in stature. A man who does or provides any of these things *for* this woman may be very attractive to her. Recognize that it is *not* the man specifically that she is gravitating to. It is the security *trait* in this case that *she* sees in him that is attractive. A want or need that *she* has that *she* wants to be filled.

Women and men often speak in terms of what a person has to *do* for them to gain their affection or love. "He needs to pay my bills!" "She needs to give me sex whenever I want it!" "I want someone who will spend time with me!" "Without finance, there's no romance!" "I need my needs to be met!"

What does any of this have to do with unconditional love for another person? Isn't unconditional love the alleged goal of a relationship?

Everyone has wants and needs that they *believe* can only be received from another person or thing. This is common. However, what is uncommon is the realization of the impact that this *mistaken idea* has on relationships. No one is actually in love with anyone. Nor do people seek relationships with people for love's sake. People are attracted to others that have the specific *traits* that they believe will satisfy *their* wants/needs and desires. These *traits* are the magnet; NOT the person. This is why relationships end when fulfillment of wants/needs and desires stops. The person was never actually loved. Only what the person did or provided to the other was loved.

If your love of me depends on what I *do* for you, can you honestly say that this is loving *me*? Of course not! It has nothing to do with me. It has everything to do with what I ***do for YOU!*** As soon as I stop doing these things, then your reason to love me stops as well. And this is what happens. Relationships falter and stop. It may not happen suddenly in a sense that you dump the person immediately. It creeps in through language such as, ***"I don't feel the way I used to, he/she has changed."*** This language is used because people are not consciously aware of what is happening. A person does not feel the same way because a change in the relationship has occurred. The other person has stopped consciously or unconsciously doing something that was done previously. One person has stopped fulfilling the other's wants/needs. It is at this point that the once believed feeling of love begins to wane.

Unfortunately, people do not recognize that they are becoming unhappy because their want/need is no longer met. They mistakenly think it is their mate that they are no longer in love with. Since they have equated love with the fulfillment of a want/need by this person, then they slowly fall out of love with the person not realizing it is not the person but the want/need that has stopped being fulfilled.

Think about all of the reasons that you have had as a basis for loving/liking another person. Isn't it all based upon what the other person does for you? A want/need or desire that you have? She "makes you feel good." He "makes you feel sexy." She "takes care of me." There are many others. Aren't all of these a reflection of what *you* got out of the relationship and are no longer getting? Look at this further and look at the circumstance surrounding the demise of the relationship. Why did any of your relationships fail? Why did you fall out love? Was it because you stopped loving the person? Or did you stop loving the person because they stopped doing or providing you with something which you received previously? Can you honestly say that you ever loved your mate? Or did you love the things they did for you?

More could be said on this, but I think you get the point. If what is called Love in a relationship today was actually unconditional love, then the love for a person would transcend what they do or do not do for you. You would love unconditionally. Of course, your mate would do things for you that fulfill your wants/needs or desires; however, the relationship would not depend on this.

Unconditional Love actually allows two people to grow together over time. But this is not what happens. We forget that everyone changes, grows and evolves. We also forget or don't realize that as a person evolves, he/she may not consciously or unconsciously want to do the same things for their mate that they did previously— things which have been equated with "love." As long as love is equated with things done by another for *me*, then it is just a matter of time before people fall out of love. People are going to change and evolve, and they are not going to continue doing the same things tomorrow that they did today. The only constant in life is <u>change</u>. Nothing stays the same. So the present mindset (*impression*) about relationships as discussed in this chapter dooms relationships to failure. Clearly another *idea* about relationships needs to be developed. An idea that is not based upon a self–centered what-have-you-done-for-me-lately mentality. An idea that promotes an actual unconditional type of love relationship.[8]

You may be thinking that from here on out you will "be" different in your relationships. This is another way of saying that you will "choose" to act differently. Well that sounds easy enough. But it takes a little bit more than simply choosing something different when all you are accustomed to doing is something else.

Do you know anyone who has not wanted to take what they have learned from a previous relationship into a new one to improve it? Does this work? Don't people seem to continue having relationships that end up in frustration and discontent no matter how many different "choices" they make?

Choice by itself does not work when dealing with an ingrained way of being. The following illustration will show you why.

---

[8] For more on this topic, see the book YOU! Are Responsible For Your Life! By Lawrence R. Mathews.

We have grown up thinking that the color of grass is green. I do not know if anyone ever specifically told you that grass was green. Nobody told me it was. But ever since I can remember, it has ALWAYS been this color. Now you are well aware, that the color we call green is that color not because of its truth, but because someone at some point in time said "this is green, therefore grass is green." There is no inherent truth in the proposition that grass is green because this same someone could have said it was yellow, or blue or pink. Had this been the case our present idea of the color of grass would reflect this different color.

So if I tell you that as of today, you can "choose" for grass to be a color other than green do you really have a choice? How can you choose when the underlying basis of your belief system has ALWAYS been that grass is green? Any so-called choice with this "green" as the base is a choice in word only. Any so called choice in this environment will be *"colored"* by the underlying belief that we have about its color. We may say with our mouths that the new color is blue, but in our hearts/mind we will still **believe** that it is green. There is an **impression** that grass is green that has been ratified and never questioned all of our lives. This green **impression** must first be *cleansed* before any real choice can be made. Any other way will have a person attempting to NOT believe that the grass is green instead of actually believing in the new choice that has been made.

The task of creating a new way of thinking and being about relationships requires us to first come to grips with our present ideas (***impressions***) about relationships and then go about the business of *cleansing* these from our minds/hearts. Then, and only then, will we be able to make an actual choice.

Clearly the present ***idea*** about relationships in the African-American community does not work for our betterment. I believe that as Black men we should initiate the process that will begin the cleansing of this false idea. Then we should present to you, (Sisters) a new idea about the purpose of relationships based upon a foundation of unconditional love. With these objectives in mind, we will determine what we as a people think and believe concerning relationships from our perspective.

The next Chapter (8) presents an example of a typical ***impression*** led relationship. These types of relationships are recipes for disaster and lead to the typical heartache and frustration common in our community. Chapter 9 presents a new "practice" and way of being in relationships. This chapter sets forth a new "purpose" for relationships based upon unconditional love. It is a new way to view and engage in relationships "from my point of view."

Chapter 8

A Typical *Impression*-Led Relationship (A practice of the relationship which IS a recipe for disaster!)

The following is a brief description of a typical relationship and how it starts and ends in our community—a relationship driven by unconscious *impressions* centered on what the other person is doing for **me** to satisfy **my** perceived wants and needs.

A man and woman meet based upon a mutual attraction. We are attracted to you for the obvious reasons, (looks, body etc.) but also for other reasons as well. We can tell that you are confident and self-assured. This confidence that you exude "turns us on" as much as your looks. **We** "feel" good (ego) by having you with us.

You are attracted to us as well. We may or may not have the specific look or body that you prefer but we carry additional qualities too. You sense from us an air of strength and confidence. You see in us a strong Black man. This perceived strength is a turn on for you as much as our looks. This perception fulfills **your** need to feel secure. (ego)

We begin dating and everything goes well. We take you out and show you a good time. **You** have fun. **You** get used to having this type of fun with us. This fun satisfies **your** need for companionship and makes **you** happy. Resultantly, you begin to look at us differently. To a certain extent, you admire us and look up to us. We feel this energy and we then **feel** like "a man!" **We feel** great because **we** have a need to please you.

The cycle that leads to the demise of the relationship has now begun. Both people will now begin to equate the feelings that develop within them with the satisfaction of having their wants and/or needs met. Unfortunately neither person realizes that as soon as we equate happiness to satisfaction of a want, automatically we will associate unhappiness to the unsatisfaction of not having that want fulfilled.

Very soon thereafter we have sex and a new bond develops. "I" becomes "We" and the relationship moves forward. Sex from your perspective makes us closer. You then begin wanting to know the inner side of us. You want us to share with you our intimate thoughts and feelings. Like all men, we have been educated not to communicate inner personal feelings. We talk a lot, but say very little. We talk about certain aspects of our business, some world events, things in the news possibly, but hardly ever, if ever, do we share with you our innermost self.

This lack of communication frustrates you. The sex has now made you feel a deeper connection with us. You want to know everything about us. You then share much (everything) about yourself hoping that we will reciprocate. We don't, not because we do not want to, but because we can't. We literally cannot and are at a loss to explain why. In fact, we do not realize that we can't. For most of us, the inner aspect of ourselves is something that we have never thought about. You question us further about ourselves, and we continually have nothing to say. When pressed about why we are not communicating with you, we respond with "that's just the way I am!"

When we don't reciprocate by expressing our feelings, you become upset in a very subtle way. You do not become angry or outwardly upset. Inwardly you wish that we would communicate with you. Communication is your security blanket. If we talk to you, there is a basis for you to be secure in knowing that we care about you. When we don't talk, you have no basis to conclude anything except that we don't care. You may even take the position that we do not talk because there is something wrong with you. Your frustration with our lack of communication grows, but because it is subtle, you do not recognize it.

This constant questioning by you about us not communicating begins to take a toll on us as well. We perceive your consistent questioning as "nagging." How many different ways do you want us to tell you that we do not have anything to talk about? Since we really have never thought about the deeper aspects of ourselves, we literally have nothing to say. *We* now begin to become frustrated. However, our frustration does not play out in subtle ways like yours. We tell you directly, to "stop nagging" about this. We may even tell you that you are getting on our nerves. This does not help the situation because from your perspective, you just want to be closer to us.

Sensing that the relationship has potential, both of us are willing to do what's necessary to make it work. One of the few aspects of our life that we will talk about, (that we *can* talk about) is our business. There are no specifics just generalities because we are attempting to show you a softer side for the betterment of the relationship. We tell you about a problem or two within our business that needs to be addressed. We may even ask you for your advice.

As soon as you find out about the problem, your independent way of "fixing things" mindset takes over. (***Impression***) You are willing to help us for the betterment of the relationship. We are a couple in this together so why wouldn't you be helpful? You volunteer to help us. It could be with credit, money or any number of things. You do this willingly. As soon as you offer to help, our "unconditional love for us" ***impression*** takes over. The ***impression*** of always having women (mothers and sisters) who take care of us no matter what. In other words unconditionally. We accept the offer even though we did not tell you about the business problem for your help. We told you this in an attempt to communicate.

The cycle that leads to the deterioration of the relationship is now in full force—a cycle that may have begun within two weeks to a month of the start of the relationship. Your *impression* and ours begin to butt heads. You have now begun to "fix" things "for" us—a fixing mentality that you have had since you were a child. You step right into this way of being as this is what you are accustomed to doing. We accept these things from you because this is what we are used to. We have always had women providing for us (mothers, sisters, other girlfriends) in a number of ways.

Your help for us grows simultaneously with our acceptance of the help. The more you help us, the more you begin to internally question the strength and independence you saw from us at the beginning. You have helped us a lot now, and we are not repaying you. You begin to subtly see us differently. We do not appear so strong anymore. In fact, we are beginning to seem rather weak. You feel like we always need to be rescued by you. The perceived thought that you could find security with us has now completely faded away. Unconsciously and subtly, you begin to dislike us. Not in an overt way but internally. You then begin questioning our judgment on small things like car directions and types of restaurants. Any mistake by us now becomes magnified by you because you now have begun to see us "differently." We are no longer seen by you as strong. You now have begun seeing us as weak.

As we accept your so-called "unconditional gifts," a negative subtle change occurs for us as well. The more we get from you in terms of things that we did not ask for, the more you begin looking like every other woman in the street that we have known. We too begin to lose respect for you. Instead of the confident and smart woman we saw previously, we begin to subconsciously see you as stupid since you are now acting like every other woman that we have known.

Unconsciously we put you on a pedestal. In our mind you are different from all other women. Unconsciously we take you off of the pedestal. You are now no different from any other woman.

These feelings are subtle from both us and are not easily recognized. Over a period of months and years the frustrated feelings intensify. Unfortunately they do not manifest in recognizable ways. For sisters, they seem to manifest in the development of unhappy feelings. You cannot explain why you are unhappy. You just are. They manifest in the development of feelings of discontent. You cannot explain why you are discontent, you just are. You stop liking us and begin to dislike us. If you are asked why, you cannot explain it. You respond "because I do." Over a two to five-year period (at most but often sooner) you become generally frustrated with the relationship. Many times this will happen right in front of your eyes, and you will still not know "why" it happened.

For us the manifestation differs. Since we do not get our "feeling" of manhood from you anymore, we are left with two choices. Get this "feeling" in the streets with other women or internalize the "feeling of inadequacy" of not "feeling" like a man. Many of us cheat because we derive our sense of manhood from our sexual prowess. We want to do this with you our woman/wife but when you stop seeing us like the man you saw at the beginning of the relationship, we will get it elsewhere. For those who want to remain true to their vows, they are in a difficult place. They remain in an environment that further erodes their sense of manhood that was limited from the beginning. Poor self esteem and a lack of confidence follow this man.

It is now a short matter of time before this relationship will end. Mentally and emotionally it already has. Both people may stay together for other reasons, but by now we are content to roam the streets and you do the same. There is a reason why there is a 49% divorce rate for first time marriages.

The failure to recognize the impact of *impressions* in relationships dooms them to failure—a failure that is promised before the relationship starts.

It is no wonder that the current practices in relationships are recipes for disaster!

"A Black Man, My Point of View"

Chapter 9

A Better Way!

There is an old saying that goes, "doing the same thing over and over again while expecting a different result is a form of insanity." To have the relationships that we desire requires us to *act* differently by viewing relationships from a different perspective than we do presently. This Chapter discusses a method (A Better Way!) that I believe will allow a couple to have the relationship that they want.

To fully digest this method people need to become **totally** aware of several things when considering becoming involved in a relationship.

• First, people must **totally** be aware that all people change over time. People mature and their wants and needs change. As they change their conscious or unconscious desire to satisfy their mates wants and needs **will** change also. This has nothing to do with the other person. It is a sign of being alive.

• Second, in a relationship two people become mirrors for each other. This means that just being in the relationship will expose each person's strengths and weaknesses. This exposure is difficult to see. Without a **total** awareness of this dynamic, people may easily associate the new difficulty in the relationship as being a problem with their mate.

●   Third, people need to be **totally** aware that they are attracted to the *soul/spirit* in their mate but becomes involved in a relationship with them because of what the other person <u>*does for them*</u>.

People Change Over Time!

Everything changes. Nothing stays the same. Even people change. Therefore in a relationship, it would seem wise to expect your mate to change over time. However, we do the opposite. We expect our mates to the stay the same. When they don't, we get mad at them or become unhappy.

Why not embrace each moment today and expect the change that is soon to come? As long as we expect it, we will prevent ourselves from considering our mates wrong for not treating us the same in the future. Additionally, this new way of thinking will eliminate the feeling of falling out of love with our mate since the underlying basis for having the feeling has been eradicated.

People are Mirrors for Each Other

It has been my experience in relationships that problems with our mates/spouse are actually problems in us. When relationships become rocky we say that the other person is the problem in the relationship. We say that we made a poor choice, and we just need to find the "right" person the next time. Very little attention is given to the role that WE play in the deterioration of the relationship.

What if the problems people have with their mate were actually **mistaken ideas** about how the other person *should be?*

Relationships are mirrors that allow you to see the inner aspect of yourself everyday. These aspects are the strengths and weakness of your personality. This is a wonderful thing! But for the relationship, a person would never to get to know the inner aspect of their being. The relationship brings that out. The current view of relationships sets people up to blame their mate for what may be their own issue. This view does not leave room for acceptance of personal responsibility. This current view can only assess blame. This of course leads to upset feelings, pain, anguish, and so on and so on......

However, the realization that I can learn about my inner strengths and weaknesses through the relationship allows an entirely different type of relationship to be created—the kind that most people speak of and desire. A relationship that is complete and fulfilling!

> # People are attracted to the soul/spirit
> # in the other person

Have you ever seen someone that was attractive to you and the attraction was beyond explanation? This particular person was not your type. They did not dress the way you wanted them to. They were too big or too small yet there was *something* about them.

There are two types of attractions. The first is not explainable. The second is the attraction based upon what a person has *identified* as attractive. An example of *identification* in the African-American male community is a woman having a "big butt". This identification is so strong that a "big butt" for some men is all they need to turn them on. An example of an *identification* for women is a man who is "buff". The term *identification* is used in this example because it is something that people accept as true because of conditioning. I can remember as a small child hearing the older boys and men speak positively about the "onion shape" rear end of a sister. I heard this type of talk long before I knew what an onion or butt was. It was inevitable that I too would come to see this body part shape as something attractive. This type of attraction is not real. It is created.

The first type of attraction is the most important. This attraction happens from the inner place of the being. In this scenario, the person is attracted to the "higher aspect" of the other. Some call this aspect the soul or spirit. It is the most important because everyone at their base is composed of this soul or spirit. Some call it energy, or consciousness, but whatever you may call it, we all have it. I believe this is where the term "soul mate" originates. You can see that this type of attraction is the most important since the attraction rarely takes on the form of your desired interest. It is beyond that. It is beyond the senses. It is this dynamic that makes it difficult to understand.

A Better Way!

You and your potential mate—prior to seriously dating—can decide that the both of you are going to help each other discover the hidden aspects of each other's personality so that the weaknesses can be turned into strengths. You and your mate can look at the relationship as a means for discovering aspects of yourself that you previously did not know were there. You and your mate can then shift your **idea** about the relationship to having it become a vehicle in which you and your mate help each other become better people. You and your mate can see each other as spiritual beings and help each other develop the inner spiritual aspect of each other's being.

What would happen if you and your mate were to be in a relationship in this way? Soon a consciousness shift would occur. The impact of your mate's behavior on you would quickly lessen—in short, you would not get as upset about the little things that annoy couples.

(underwear being left on the floor.) Whether or not she put out would be less important since your seeing the spiritual aspect of your mate would unconsciously identify you with your mate's spiritual self. This consciousness shift would lessen the impact of your feeling like something wrong is happening.

Relationships are the perfect vehicle for becoming better people. A mate is a mirror for you, and through the relationship, if you look, you get to see yourself in a way that you don't see while single. This is a great opportunity to grow. When growth occurs, it becomes easy to live life spiritually, because you become less and less caught up in feeling bad about not having your wants/needs and desires met.

I don't think for a moment that anyone wants to feel bad when their relationship starts changing for the worse—a change that creates ultimately nothing but pain, frustration, hurt, rejection and a lot of other stuff. We have it backwards folks! We go into relationships in a way that is designed to make us more hurt and more frustrated. Whether we like it or not, whether we face it or not, whether we bury our heads in the sand or not, once we become involved in a relationship **all** of our weaknesses are going to come to the surface.

When these weakness show up, we blame the other person and immediately begin feeling bad. The situation then goes from bad to worse.

Why not accept that the relationship is going to bring up aspects of ourselves that we probably will not like? Why not do this in the context of being with a mate who wants to be with you, who is willing to work with you on those aspects? These aspects can be obstacles to having a complete and fulfilling relationship. And if you allow them to be, they are obstacles to seeing what's right in front of you: a person that can help you while you help them become the highest form of person there is; a spiritual person having a human experience!

What would be gained by adopting this new way of being in relationship? First, you would get a mate who would be considerate of your shortcomings since the relationship would be founded upon the recognition that each person has them. Therefore, you would immediately bring compassion into the relationship and simultaneously remove contempt. You would also get a mate with a growing sense of patience with themselves and with you since they would realize that this new idea about the relationship would take time to master.

Something else happens in this process. A different type of love develops. A deeper one. As you begin to see the spiritual aspect of your mate on a regular basis, your love for them grows beyond the outer exterior of the person, their body. You grow to love the higher aspect of them. Their soul/spirit. You know that the soul/spirit itself is eternal. Therefore, as you begin to love the soul in your mate, the love that develops becomes an eternal one. This love of the soul is a love that people in this society do not experience. Frankly, it is not possible to achieve this type of love, the way relationships are presently practiced.

Who doesn't want eternal love?

Eternal love transcends the puppy-love-feel-good type of love. It is the type of love that once perfected is always present. This type of love does NOT mean that a couple will always stay together. They may decide for whatever reason, that some day it is best for them to part. But this eternal type love always remains. Therefore, there is no bitterness at the time of breaking up, or very little compared with break-ups of relationships during our era.

So I ask, why in the area of romance do we continue to do the same things over and over again when clearly it is not working?

A new **idea** has been presented. A new way of thinking about relationships. This new **idea** can be used for a new couple or for a couple who have been together for a while. It will work most effectively though in a new relationship, as this can be the foundation for the launch of the relationship. In a relationship that is already established, people may be too deeply entrenched in their positions of who is right versus who is wrong. If this is the case, it may actually be in a person's best interest to start all over again in another relationship. A great deal of psychological damage occurs in an unhappy relationship.

For an older relationship, lots of patience, lots of time and lots of effort to practice this new way of thinking will be needed. This extra effort may not be something both people want, when they are entrenched in their views of who is right and who is wrong.

This new **idea** of relationships may not be something you agree with. If not, develop a new way of approaching a relationship for yourself, see if your potential mate buys into it, and then the both of you develop your relationship around this new ideal.

When a new **idea** about relationships is fostered and developed, relationships will become actual vehicles for a love that will promote the spiritual development in a person. An eternal love.

"A Black Man, My Point of View"

SECTION 4

BRINGING IT ALL HOME!

*"Do Not Allow What You Think,
Or The Way You Think To
<u>Limit</u>
What You Think,
Or The Way You Think!"*

Anpu Waset

Chapter 10

The Best Way to Use this Book (Summary)

To get the most benefit from this book, you need to recognize the key points that we have discussed.

You should have no doubt that the current practices in relationships today *are* recipes for disaster! The current "practices are built on a "what have you done for me lately" mentality. As you engage in actions that satisfy the wants/needs and desires of your partner, a good "feeling" is generated in the body. This "feeling" is so strong that it can cause your mate to not want to sleep, eat or drink. This "feeling" is equated with Love. Love is mistakenly equated with <u>*actions done for them*</u> to satisfy their wants and/or needs. Love based upon "what" someone does for you is not love at all. It is a severe form of egoism.

Wants and needs that *"drive"* you (especially in relationships) often derive from centuries old *unconscious **impressions***. Although you may think that your desires are born from like/dislike type of choices, the opposite can be true.

Since the only constant in life is change, it is only a short matter of time before the person who has become the object of your affections consciously or unconsciously stops fulfilling your wants and needs. As we change we do not purposely stop doing the things that we did previously. There are a lot of reasons for this shift in action. Suffice it to say that as we grow and change, our actions grow and change as well. If we equate Love with the fulfillment of our wants and needs, Love will soon fade away as the actions that were the basis of Love change or stop altogether.

A new relationship "practice" is needed. However, until we are ready to tackle the reality of the present day state of relationship affairs, we each should be aware of the drivers of our own personality and those of our mate.

Black men are driven by their unconscious desire to "feel" like men. Manhood, as defined by this society is the man's ability to provide and support his family. This has been difficult in a society not created by Black men for Black men and the opportunities for us have been limited. Couple this with the unconscious *impressions* of "insecurity" and "personal inferiority" handed down from generation to generation since the days of the plantation, and you have a very interesting personality to deal with.

Black women are driven by their unconscious desire to feel "secure." To compensate for the "feeling of insecurity," she is taught to be strong and independent. Women are taught that they do not need men. It's has gotten so bad today that women openly discuss becoming lesbians because they say they do not need us or because we have so many communication problems, that there's no use in dealing with us. The strong and independent mindset in a relationship will tend to emasculate whatever man she is with. Couple this with unconscious *"impressions"* of wanting "unconditional love" handed down from generation to generation since the days of the plantation, and you again have an interesting personality to deal with.

The information in this book will not suddenly turn your mate into the person of your dreams. This means that your treating your man like a "man" may not make him go out and get a job and support his family if he was not doing so already. Nor will providing "total financial support" to the strong Black woman stop her from her emasculating tendencies. What this information allows you to do is have a different context for understanding your mate when a situation in the relationship develops.

Since there are two sides to every story, awareness of the drivers of your mate's personality allows you to see the new situation from the eyes of this "driver." It's like putting on a pair of glasses and viewing the situation from this new perspective. Actually, it is like putting on a pair of x-ray glasses. Now your view of the situation will transcend the outer appearance of the situation and allow you to see it from a deeper perspective. I sincerely believe that the drivers I describe are prevalent in ALL Black men and women. The degree of the *"impressions"* may differ, but the state of mind is the same for everyone. All men no matter what you "see," are driven by the same things and so are women.

Once this is understood, situations that develop in the relationship can be viewed from the perspective of the drivers of your mates' personality. Then a decision can be made on how best to deal with the situation. With this new perspective, a new action may be necessary. Or it might be best to do nothing at all. This will depend on the situation and the personality type of you and your mate. However, what this *will* do is shift the mindset and prevent you from thinking of your mates' actions as personal slights. Since they are being driven by their unconscious wants/needs and desires, their conduct towards you is not personal at all. It is internal. This is easy to see when viewed from this new perspective. However, it is almost impossible to do when love is equated with giving me my wants/needs and desires. From this vantage point, actions of the other person can be nothing but personal.

It is the intent of this book to shift the relationship conversation from one of "what have you done for me lately" to one of unconditional love. Has anyone yet tired of being frustrated, hurt, upset and all of the other feelings that happen over and over and over and over again? There has to be a "Better Way." It is time to end the present practices in relationships. This is especially true when you consider that these are practices that we had no input in when they were developed. These are the practices of relationships from the European, Western world perspective. Frankly they don't work for them and they definitely don't work for us. Are you yet sick and tired of being sick and tired of getting the same results in every relationship?

"A Black Man, My Point of View"

Chapter 11

Solutions

This Chapter provides solutions that can be used when dealing with current relationship dramas. However, you should be aware that solutions to problems do NOT solve the problem without a necessary ingredient being in place *first.*

Solutions are not helpful unless a person wanting the solution has become "*sick and tired of being sick and tired*" of having the problem in the *first place*.

Until this state of mind has been reached, solutions come in one ear and go right out the other. People will "listen" to what is said, but will NOT "hear" any of it. The dynamic is similar to an alcoholic who will not admit he has a drinking problem. As his family member, you can tell him (solution) what he should do. Until he admits that he has a drinking problem, (which occurs after he has become "*sick and tired of being sick and tired*" of being an alcoholic), nothing is going to change. He needs to reach a place where he has had enough! Until then, giving him a solution is not going to help. Therefore, solutions for anyone who has not reached his/her limit will do little if any good.

In the realm of relationships, we also have to reach that state of being "*sick and tired of being sick and* _tired._" It is amazing how many people that do the same thing over and over again in relationships think that eventually they will find the "right" person all the while enduring the same heartache, pain and frustration. They overemphasize the brief moments of jubilation and severely underemphasize the long-lasting moments of heartache and pain. They then place the blame on choosing the "wrong" person. Once the "right" person is found, people believe that things will be better. Since time waits for no man or woman, people look up and find themselves 45 years old and older still waiting for Mr. or Mrs. Right. Unfortunately these people have not yet reached their limit. They continue doing the same thing over and over again. The behavior is much like that of the alcoholic who is addicted to alcohol. You could say that the person who does the same thing over and over again in relationships is also addicted. They are addicted to the "feeling of heartache, pain and frustration." This analogy may seem a bit odd, but reflection on it will show the wisdom behind it. Very few addictions are good for the body or mind of a person. Alcohol is bad for the body and mind and hurts them both in many ways. The same old relationship drama that leads to heartache and pain is a different kind of hurt but a hurt nevertheless. Since neither the alcoholic nor the relationship drama "king/queen" can stop doing the same thing over and over again, you could say that both are addicted.

Solutions to problems require first an admission that there is a problem and then that you have had enough of it. You must be _sick and tired of being sick of tired of the problem_ to benefit from any solution!

If you are _sick and tired of being sick and tired_ of the same old relationship drama, here are some solution methods for you:

1. <u>Read this book one more time objectively with your mate!</u>

It has been my experience that people tend to be defensive when questioned about their actions. People look for ways to validate what was done and how it was done. This is unfortunate because no growth can occur when a person is defensive. This happens quite a bit in relationships especially as women question men about why we did or did not do something. Therefore, this book should be read again with your mate from an objective point of view. The male should read the book from the perspective of the woman and the woman should read the book from the perspective of the man. There is no longer a need to discuss what's wrong with the other gender in the traditional sense, unless you want a traditional type of relationship that creates heartache, frustration and pain. It is better to look at the male/female relationship from the other person's perspective and then discuss ways that your relationship can be improved from this space. It took me quite awhile to "see" a women's perspective outside of my own male bias. I am still in the process of working through my inability to "see" outside of my own viewpoint. This is necessary though, because both men and women will continue to support their version of what is the problem in the relationship, (the other person) as long as they do not look at it objectively. Read the book again and pay special attention to Chapters 5-9.

2. <u>Sisters, accept that Black men think differently from you!</u>

An argument can be made that sisters want us to think like sisters. This is interesting because you do not appear to have this expectation from other groups of people. You don't expect White men or other ethnic groups to think like you. However, with us, this appears to be what you want. It seems clear that overall you think that you are smarter than us. Therefore, our comments or suggestions do not resonate with you unless they are in accord with what you already think or they come from someone that you trust. Accept us for who we are (strengths and weaknesses) and how we think (differently from you). Contrary to what you may believe, you are not perfect.

3. <u>Brothers, recognize that sisters have a NEED to trust us!</u>

Contrary to what we were taught growing up, sisters actually do want the truth from us no matter what that is. Trust is actually a code word for security. Women feel secure when they can rely on what we say. That means we are dependable. Women have a need for security from us. They have had this need since the days of the plantation and nothing has changed since then. Telling women the truth even when it may seem stupid from our perspective, allows the woman to feel secure.

We as men have a tendency of isolating a specific issue and getting caught up in everything it entails. However our sisters are more concerned with being able to trust what we say. We are often correct in thinking that women will adversely react to particular issues. We err though in "seeing" the issue in its context of the big picture. Women also "see" the specific issue in the context of the big picture. Both pictures are not the same. The big picture for women is trust and according to the sisters who have contributed to this work, this is the most important relationship issue for them. So we must be COMPLETELY honest with them at ALL TIMES!

4. **<u>Sisters, listen to what we say, not what you want to hear!</u>**

Although we as men are not the best communicators, if you listen to us objectively, you will learn a lot. Subjective listening blocks any information that is contrary to what the listener is listening for. If you listen for only what you want to hear, you will hear *nothing* that is being said. We tell women all the time how we feel. We just don't say it with words. We say it with our actions.

5. <u>**Brothers, we must do everything we say we'll do without fail!**</u>

Dependability is very important. This is another offshoot of security. Dependability is especially important for a sister who has never consistently been able to depend on anyone other than herself. To establish a new and higher order within the relationship we must act differently. We must do everything we say we'll do and when we can't, we must communicate this to our mates as soon as possible so the situation can be addressed. *We must do as we say!*

6. <u>**Sisters, trust our judgment. No matter what!**</u>

Have you ever noticed that we as Black men have no problem trusting your judgment on matters? Have you noticed that even when your judgment is "faulty" and does not turn out well, that we do not blame you for the poor decision? We roll with the consequences and keep on going. We do not remind you weeks, months or years later about a poor decision that you may have made. Under most circumstances you are reluctant to trust our judgment. When you do decide to trust us, God forbid our decision is poor. For the rest of the relationship we will always be reminded by you of the mistake/s we made. Of course this leads to us slowly but surely removing ourselves from the decision-making process. The fewer decisions we make, the more we are accused of lacking initiative. This leads to a lessening of respect for us. How can you respect someone who doesn't have any initiative? Treat us the same way we treat you. Trust us in decision making, and if it does not turn out the way you expected, roll with it like we do with you.

7. <u>Brothers, make a point of earning our sisters' respect.</u>

As Black men we want the respect of our women. Based on my communications with the sisters who have contributed to this work, Black Women want to respect us. Therefore, this should be an easy solution. Unfortunately it is not. People are so accustomed to defending their position in the relationship that there is no room left for anything else. Positions are defended in these types of ways. Men will say, "women nag too much, they can't make up their minds, are never satisfied and can't handle the truth." Women say other things such as, "all men are dogs; you can't trust any of them, and that there cannot be any romance without finance." All these kinds of statements justify keeping a person in the same position at all times. It places the problem outside of yourself and over there on your mate. Therefore you have nothing to do but put up with your mate. This mindset blames the other person and sees them as the problem. There is no room to see how YOU may be the cause of the specific relationship drama occurring at the moment.

You can see how this keeps people stuck in the same behavior patterns. We will gain the respect of our women when we make the first move and step outside of the same "old way" of being. When we do this, I believe that our women will reciprocate and respond accordingly.

8. <u>Sisters, support us mentally and emotionally.</u>

We as Black men have a need to "feel" like men. You can help us to get this feeling in small ways that cost nothing—a kind word and encouragement. In essence, believe in us. These actions can be done easily mentally and emotionally. The easiest way for you to do this is by actually *believing* in us. Believing that we can move mountains. Believing that we can and will take care of business. We want to take care of our woman. We will do anything for you when you believe in us. Mental and emotional support is easy if you have confidence in us and actually believe in us. However, this type of support is impossible from you if you do not have confidence in our abilities. If you are with a man who you have little or no confidence in, then it is probably best for the both of you to not be in a relationship together. He cannot "feel" like a man with a woman who does not believe in him. You cannot respect a man that you lack confidence in. A positive relationship cannot flourish in this type of environment.

9. <u>Brothers, initiate actions within the relationship to improve it.</u>

More than anything I have heard from sisters in discussions about relationships is that they want us to initiate actions within the relationship. Whether this is the complete planning of a vacation or development of an idea about how to save money for the kid's college education, sisters do not want to feel like they are responsible for having to come up with all of the ideas to better the relationship. It doesn't matter what we come up with; they want us to initiate more. This makes sense given their having-to-do-everything life experience. They want us to handle the business, and this is reflected in our taking initiative within the relationship.

10. <u>Sisters, keep your checkbook in your purse</u>

Often you are quick to help us financially, providing this "help" even though we do not ask for it. Often you volunteer your credit card or money when we present you with a problem or situation. What happens? We never repay you. Why? Because your money is not what we need. Money is actually support from you. Since we have a need to support you and not be supported by you, we cannot feel like men when you constantly provide for us in this way. The action of providing for men financially is not good for us, nor is it good for women. It does not take long for women to start wanting (needing) their money back. When it is not given back, loss of respect for your man soon follows. It is not the end of the relationship, but it is the beginning of the end of "seeing" this man the same way that you did previously.

To be clear, I am not advocating a wholesale curtailment of helping your mate when he is in need. That is not the point. But the time has long passed for women to be working two jobs and taking care of all the bills and kids, while the man stays home and writes lyrics to songs or music to pursue his dreams. The pursuit of a dream should occur AFTER you get home from work unless you don't mind pursuing your dream while living in your car or a homeless shelter.

Of course, if you give us your money, we will spend it. However, we do not need your money. We need your support. Any woman that is with a man that needs her money and not her support is with the wrong man.

11. <u>Brothers & Sisters resist acting on your *unconscious impressions*.</u>

This book has gone into great detail to bring awareness of the unconscious *"impressions"* driving both male and female personalities.

Now that you are aware of them, work on moving beyond them in the relationship. Objectively looking at the situation through the eyes of your partner will allow this to happen.

12. <u>Sisters, recognize that it's Ok to be a woman.</u>

The world has changed a lot since I was a younger man. I recall a time that Black woman did not tolerate being disrespected by anyone. What happened? Today it seems like the number of women who like being treated like women is dwindling rapidly. Especially in the generation of women who are 30 years old and younger.

Today it appears that women no longer like the old fashioned way of being when men used to "court" a woman: having doors opened for you, receiving flowers and tokens of appreciation. Men have no problem doing these types of things, but these types of actions do not appear to be important to women anymore.

Today the younger generation of women is in videos wearing little to no clothing while men parade around them like they are sex objects. Women allow men to address them outside of their name (whore, bitch) and it seems like these words have become terms of endearment. I recall there was a time when only "certain types of women" would date the dope man or the hustler. Now it seems like every women will do this. What happened?

Sisters, you have voluntarily given away your womanhood. At some point women accepted being treated with what I call disrespect by men. This has been a big change from the women of earlier times who would not accept this type of behavior. Sisters do not forget that we are the pursuers of you. We will do what we have to do to be with you. If you demand to be treated like a woman we will respond accordingly. Today it is allowable to call you outside of your name. If this was not acceptable, we would stop.

It appears as if the desire for a "rough neck bad boy" has taken over in our community. Nice guys today finish last. What do you think happens when men realize that women don't like nice guys? They become "rough neck bad boys!" If we want the girl who likes "rough necks," why should we act any other way?

I believe that you want to be treated like a Queen. We want to treat you like a Queen. Accept the fact that it is ok to be a woman and expect nothing short of that. You will be glad you did.

13. <u>Sisters, accept that you want a strong Black man and get out of the way.</u>

Sisters, aren't you tired of bringing home all of the bacon, frying it up in a pan, taking care of the kids and everything else that needs to be done? Aren't you tired of holding it down by yourself? Are you ready for someone else to pick up the slack now? If not, you should be because you have held it down for far too long. Sisters stop and take a long look in the mirror and reflect on these words: You say you want a strong black man, but is this really true?

What would a strong black man look like to you? How would he act and how would he be? Would he be decisive? Would he be confident? Would he be creative? Would he be a person who takes initiative? Would he be kind and considerate towards you? Would he take care of you emotionally, mentally, and financially? Would this describe the type of man that you would consider to be a strong black man?

If so, then think about how your conduct and behavior is with men and determine if you are accepting of this these types of behaviors from us. Or does your way of being with us block these types of behaviors from manifesting from us towards you?

The historical and present day need of Black women to be responsible for everything produces a mindset that is very controlling. This is understandable. Responsibility entails a certain level of control. However, without limits, a controlling mindset can be problematic in a relationship.

Think about this: Our confidence in our decision-making ability with you will not last long if you accept our advice only AFTER it has been validated by someone else. It will be difficult to be decisive with you if you continually remind us of every poor decision we have made. Open displays of kindness and affection to you will wane if you loudly disagree with us in public. Over time, we will forget about our own desire to take care of you financially if you constantly remind us that you do not need us for this.

We as Black men want to be strong for ourselves and you. Unfortunately there are not that many role models around. For the most part strong black men do not exist in this society, so we are all learning on the fly. Recognize how your "responsible" way of being affects this process when you deal with us. Practice makes perfect and perfect practice creates a new way of being. We want to be strong Black men. You want strong Black men. So shall it be written; so shall it be done.

Chapter 12

Conclusion

We as a people have forgotten how great we are and have been. Let's clean up our relationship drama so that today we can reach the glorious heights we once achieved.

Here is how I see it: We as Black men must develop a coordinated strategy that will allow our children to be raised in a manner that will produce adults with the types of morals and character that we deem to be important for our community.

Once developed, we then must present this strategy to the sisters for ratification. The idea of morality as espoused by Western society clearly leaves a lot to be desired. We must initiate this with you sisters, recognizing the awesome power that you have within yourselves as the group who are our children's first caregivers/teachers. You sisters, as the first teachers of children, have a tremendous influence on them. The joint harnessing of the male and female in a concerted manner has not occurred since our ancestors moved up and into Kmt (Egypt) from what is considered today as Ethiopia and the Sudan. The monuments that stand to this day in Africa are a testimony to what can be done when the male and female come together as one. All that is needed to come together is the willpower to do it. Nothing more; nothing less.

Given the state of affairs of relationships, I would think that people have tired of the same relationship drama over and over again. Even with new partners, it's the same issues and drama. When people <u>fully</u> tire of this insanity, the willpower to create something different will be there.

May the Divine bless you with Eternal Bliss and Peace!

Chapter 13

Questions & Answers

The questions below were given to me by a number of women. I have grouped those questions that are similar.

Question 1:

• **Why do Black men cheat? I know women cheat, but men cheat all the time for no reason. Women usually cheat for a reason. (Lack of love, sex and/or companionship)**

• **Why is it so easy for men to have multiple lovers and mislead each woman by telling her she's the only one he's seeing?**

• **What makes a man want to be with one woman?**

• **Why do men feel they need to have more than one woman?**

• **Why does it seem as if men enjoy sexual intercourse more than women?**

- **Why does a man cheat? Especially when he says or acts like he has what he needs at home and is in a committed relationship?**

Answer:

I listed the above questions together because they appear to be asking the same thing although in different ways. Before I delve too deeply into the answer, read Chapter 7 again, think about it for five minutes, and then come back and read this answer.

First of all, I believe that both men and women want complete and fulfilling relationships. Men want to be in a committed relationship. Once we commit, we want to be faithful to one woman. We do not want to cheat. However, we are no different from anyone else in this society when interacting with our mate in a relationship. We too have wants/needs that we want fulfilled through the relationship. We cheat when our wants and needs are not met.

The current practice in relationships is one built upon having "one person" who will fulfill your wants/needs and desires. In fact, a strong case can be made that this is the whole point of having a relationship in the first place. With that as a backdrop, recognize that the main **unconscious** want/need of a man is to *feel* like a man. Many of us are not able to articulate this. That shouldn't be surprising, since it is unconscious and because we are not good at communicating. However, the *feeling* is there and is a major driver of our actions in relationships with you. When men cheat we do so because we have stopped getting a want/need of ours met by you. When we cheat and are having sex with another woman or women, this does not mean that you have stopped having sex with us. (Although that too might be the case.) We cheat because we *feel* a certain way with this other woman that we have stopped *feeling with* you. We *feel* special and strong again with the other woman. We may *feel* like this other woman looks up to us. We may *feel* like we can do anything with her. These exact same *feelings* were there when we first met you. However, for a variety of reasons they have subsided. The lack of these "feel like a man" *feelings* with you are the reasons why we cheat. This is our **want/need or desire** that we have stopped getting from you. When this happens, we find this *"feeling"* elsewhere.

The first question in the group of questions making up Question 1, says that women unlike men cheat for a reason. That reason was stated to be for "love, companionship or sex." Aren't these reasons the **wants/needs and desires** from the woman's perspective? The wants/needs in this question are love, companionship and/or sex. A man's wants/needs or desire is to feel like a man. Both the man and woman have a want/need that they want fulfilled. A want that their mate satisfied at the beginning of their relationship but presently, for whatever reason, has stopped.

African-American's have adopted the "practice" of relationships from the culture of Western society. This "practice" is predicated on being with someone who gives you what you want when you want it. (Wants/needs) As Janet Jackson said so eloquently, it is a "what have you done for me lately mindset." As long as we get what we want, (our desires and needs met) we say we are in love. When the other person stops satisfying this want/need we say we have fallen out of love. In this setting it should not be surprising to find men cheating on women. The man who cheats is no different from anyone else in a relationship. He does what he has to do to get his needs met.

Love predicated on what you are doing or not doing for me any longer is a set up for infidelity. It is also a set up for much emotional heartache and pain, as it is the precursor for the ultimate demise of the relationship.

Men also cheat for another reason. There are no repercussions. Women do not break up with men when there is infidelity. Women get mad and may talk a lot about it, but nothing happens and the relationship continues. To a certain extent women condone their man's infidelity. How often do you hear women say "men are just dogs"? This saying is no longer just talk by women, but has become a deeply imbedded belief. Therefore, when men cheat on their woman, after the upset and anger subside, it is rare for a woman to not forgive this man. The opposite is true with men. If a man catches his woman cheating, he ends the relationship. Case closed. There is nothing to discuss. We are not tolerant of this behavior. Therefore, it does not happen as frequently. (Of course women do cheat, but they do a better job of not getting caught. For men we really don't want to be caught. But ultimately it does not matter if we are caught or not because after all is said and done you are going to take us back.)

This shows that the African-American woman may have an unconscious want/need that may be driving her in the relationship. A need to have a man. This driver explains a lot about the forgiving nature women have with men who have been unfaithful. A woman who does not want to be alone may unconsciously subject herself to treatment and behavior by a man that is unacceptable. The desire to have a want/need fulfilled is a powerful emotion that leads people to do and accept crazy things.

Men cheat because we have wants/needs and desires that we want fulfilled. Our wants are different from those of women, but they are wants nevertheless. When we stop getting our wants/needs met with you, we go someplace else. This should not come as a surprise. This is the way ALL people "practice" relationships in this society.

Question 2:

- **Why don't Black men stick around to support their children?**

- **Why don't Black men pay child support?**

Answer:

There are a couple of answers to this question, a psychological answer and a practical answer. I said before that both men and women have unconscious *impressions* that have been passed down through the generations from the days of the plantation. During the time of slavery Black men never had to be responsible for taking care of their children. Blacks were considered as property of the owner. For taxing purposes, the Africans now in the Americas were considered as 3/5ths of a human being. The "master/plantation owner" provided for the offspring of his property. So a deeply imbedded *impression* was created from that experience: the belief that all we have to do is make babies, and someone else will take care of them. It seems to me that the thinking of the Black man of today is strikingly similar to that of the Black man on the plantation.

Unfortunately, the psychological answer to the question does not help from a practical point of view. Consider this: If you sleep with a man who is not taking care of the kids he has presently, or if he is not working, or stays at home with his parents, (i.e., he is not supporting himself) why should it be surprising that this man will not provide support for a new child? In general terms, men who are responsible for themselves or the children they already have, will be responsible for new children they may have. Under certain situations these responsible men may flip the script and stop providing, (for example after a divorce) but a new mindset happens during this traumatic time that influences that change. Men who do not provide for themselves or children at the time you sleep with them will not be responsible for new children that may be born of that union. It is as simple as that.

Question 3:

- **Why don't Black men show emotion to the one they love?**

- **Why do Black men not like to cry in public?**

- **Why do men have a problem showing emotions? (crying, etc.)**

Answer:

In previous chapters in this book, it was explained that the present definition of manhood in Western society was not created by Black men for Black men. It was created by White men for White men. So Black men over the last one-hundred-and-fifty years have developed a twisted view of what being a man is. Black men do not cry or show their emotions in public, because we have identified with a definition of manhood that does not allow it.

Western society's definition of manhood has been that it is not manly to cry in public or ever show emotion. This aspect of the definition of manhood is not confined to Black men only. White men are guilty of the same thing. The inability to express emotions to a mate is not solely a Black male issue. It is a male/man issue, an issue in effect that needs a revision for all men.

Question 4:

• **Why are some men envious of a strong Black woman?**

Answer:

It is not actually envy, but more a sign of insecurity. (Although it can be both) The insecurity arises from the unconscious *impression* in Black men of wanting to *feel* like men. The definition of manhood in this society is the ability to provide for one's family. Society by and large was not designed with Black men in mind and opportunities have been limited. The fewer the opportunities the more insecurity.

This insecurity is more prevalent in a society where Black women are seen as less threatening than Black men, therefore they are hired faster for jobs than men. The work world also gets two for one by hiring a Black woman: it gets a woman and a black person. So when manhood is defined by the ability to provide for one's family, and the opportunity to do that is limited for men while more open for women, Black men's "envious" reaction to our sister's should not be surprising.

Underneath, the man is not really envious of the woman. It manifests as envy, but that is not what it is. It is actually a sense of inadequacy because of the feeling that one does not measure up. Strong here would imply the ability to provide for the family better than the man.

Some sisters make the problem worse by wearing their strength on their sleeves. They openly proclaim they don't need a man, and emasculate him. This action and behavior is also a part of the problem. It's bad enough that you make more money than him. You don't have to consistently remind him about it.

So it really is not an issue of envy. It is actually an issue of insecurity.

Question 5:

• **Why is it that men who don't have a good relationship with their mothers, mistreat the women in their life?**

• **Is how a man treats his mother a good way to measure how he will treat his woman?**

Answer:

A man's mother is the first woman that he believes loves him unconditionally. But that love is not completely unconditional. She derives her sense of motherhood from the child. But it is the closest type of unconditional love that we experience until we are ready to find a bride.

The specific answer to the question lies in the question itself. Why would a man treat any woman "better" than he treated his own mother? A person who he perceives as loving him unconditionally? Where would he practice treating a woman in a nice way without his mother? A man learns his way of being with women from his interactions with his mother. I believe men marry women who are similar in their way and being to their mothers.

A man who has a good relationship with his mother will treat his woman or wife well. A man who has an unhealthy relationship with his mother has no basis for determining how a woman should be treated. There is no telling how a man like this will treat his woman.

Men who have unhealthy relationships with their mothers should be avoided.

Question 6:

- **What is the real difference between "nagging" and repeating or reminding someone of a request?**

Answer:

What you consider to be "repeating or reminding" for us is considered "nagging." We don't want to be constantly reminded. Just because we do not always do things at the moment you want us to, does not mean we have forgotten the request hence the need to be reminded. We will get to it when we get to it. The problem lies in our not communicating to you our plan for if or when we will do it. We are poor at communication in that area. However, we do not want to be reminded because we equate reminding with telling us what to do and when. What you consider repeating or reminding is "nagging" to us because we perceive that as telling us what to do. For us there is no difference between nagging and reminding.

Question 7:

- **Are soul mates really probable/possible from a man's point of view?**

Answer:

The idea of soul mates IS possible from a man's point of view. We too want to be with our "soul mate". However, the whole idea of what a soul mate is, and how that is important in a relationship needs to be re-examined in light of reality.

Frankly the concept and idea of a soul mate is a concept that is skewed. Why is it skewed? Because people speak in terms of the soul, but spend little if any time getting to know this aspect of their being. How can anyone find their soul mate when they don't know what their soul is? What is the soul? What is it composed of? Where can it be found? What is its relationship with the other soul you want your soul to "mate" with? How should this actually be done?

I believe that what people call their "soul" is nothing more than the "good feeling emotion" derived from "getting" a want/need or desire met from another person. This *feeling* today is also referred to as Love. This *feeling* is very strong. However, this *feeling* is not the soul. It is not even Love. It is nothing but the temporary satisfaction of having a want/need met. As long as the want/need is met, "Love" is there. As soon as it ends, Love is gone. WE mistakenly place the soul in this context. But it does not belong there. When we do this, we make a mistake and do a disservice to what the soul actually is.

I believe an understanding of the soul from a male/female relationship point of view requires a basic understanding of some things about it. First, it should be recognized that people have forgotten what their soul is. People talk about the soul a great deal. Very few people have actually experienced the aspect of themselves that is their soul. Second, to experience the soul, a person needs to have an unconditioned mind.

The mind needs to be cleansed of the idea that the body and human experience is the reality whereas the soul and experiences of it are intermittent and isolated events. We have it backwards. This is what unconditioning entails. Reversing the mindset. We are not human beings having intermittent spiritual experiences. We are spiritual beings having intermittent human ones!

The soul of a person cannot be seen, touched, smelled, tasted, or heard. Yet people unsuccessfully try and use these senses to determine whether or not another person is their soul mate. But isn't the soul eternal? Isn't it infinite? The five senses are limited. Eternity cannot be seen or tasted, so this method of experiencing the soul will not work. Infinity cannot be smelled, touched or heard, so this method of experiencing the soul will not work either.

To experience the soul, you have to go to a place beyond your senses. Until that is done, you will only be talking about something (soul-mates) that you do not have a clue about.

Soul mates are NOT possible from any point of view as long as the idea of love/relationships is based on the "what-have-you-done-for-me-lately" mindset prevalent in this culture.

However it is possible for those who choose a practice in relationships centered on the idea that we are spiritual beings having a human experience!

Question 8:

- **How far should a woman go to support, encourage, or protect her man, whether he is right or wrong?**

Answer:

The issue is not a right or wrong issue. As long as you look at it from this perspective, you won't be able to support, encourage, or protect this man. Right or wrong leads to comparisons, and comparisons inevitably lead to propping certain people up while looking down at others. For example, if a woman looks at the decisions and actions of her man from the perspective of right versus wrong, she will have a basis for reminding him of the wrong decisions that were made. Rarely do women acknowledge us when we do something "right", but quite often we are reminded when we do something "wrong." So a better way of looking at this question should be considered.

The issue really is what can be done that will help the relationship prosper. The goal is to become a unit of one instead of two people. Therefore a woman should recognize the *unconscious* ***impressions*** driving a man, and a man should recognize the *unconscious **impressions*** driving you.

All we need is encouragement. We do not need women taking care of us. We need to take care of you. It is my experience that women view support and encouragement as taking care of men, like the woman works two or three jobs and raises the kids while he stays at the recording studio trying to get a record contract. This is NOT the kind of support we need, and it is out of order. If you work, we need to work as well. The support he needs is a hug or a kiss or his favorite dinner when he arrives home from a job that he can't stand—a job that he took to support his family until he finds a better one. That is support. Encouragement is believing that he will achieve his goals and dreams, goals and dreams that he is seeking to achieve "part-time" and on weekends AFTER he has gotten home from doing the work necessary to support his family.

Support and encouragement is not women taking care of men. Although many of us accept this willingly, we do not need it. We do not need surrogate mothers. We need to be men.

A disservice is done to both the man and woman when the man is not forced to at least contribute support to his family. A man who wants nothing more than to concentrate on the pursuit of his dreams to the exclusion of providing something for his family is a man that a woman has no need for. Get rid of this dead weight as quickly as possible. Don't support or encourage a man who does not do what is necessary to contribute to the support of his family.

Question 9:

- **Can a real relationship be established with a man in prison?**

Answer:

Yes. This decision, however, should be made with a great deal of care and caution. A couple of things should be considered when deciding to engage in this type of relationship. First, a woman should recognize that the unemployment rate for Black men with college degrees who are not incarcerated is very high. If a man is imprisoned for a felony, his prospects for finding employment when he gets out will be difficult at best. It is more probable that the type of employment he finds won't be enough to support him or a family. Ideally, this man should be learning a skill while incarcerated that he can use when his sentence is complete. Plumbing and carpentry are skills that a man with a felony can do for himself. His debt to society is not an issue with this type of skill. Additionally, the money made with either of these skills is very good. Supporting himself and his family with this type of income will not be difficult.

Second, a woman should realize that this man may bring an assortment of issues into the relationship after being incarcerated. This man has not taken care of himself for the time while in jail. He has had everything provided for him. He has not had to pay rent. He has not had to pay gas and electricity bills. He has not had to buy food for himself. He has become totally dependent. He may have sexual issues. This man learns no skills in jail that will help him deal with supporting himself and you. Most importantly he has had time away (the length of his incarceration) from dealing with the common issues in a male/female relationship.

Third, this man probably has anger and control issues. In jail he had to deal with a survival-of-the-strongest mentality. He may have had to use anger to survive. In this environment fighting would be common. When this man returns home, there is no switch that suddenly gives him the ability to control his emotions. All he knows is how to react to his emotions as soon as they arrive—a reaction that probably got him in trouble in the first place. It is a short matter of time before this man becomes upset and angry about his inability to find a job. It is not long before he becomes upset about the woman wearing the pants in the household and working and bringing in all the money. This man can easily break and become abusive. It won't be long before this man may feel forced to go back to crime as a way to provide for himself. With a record and no skill or trade, what other choices does he have?

Sisters, you may have the belief that you can "fix" this situation. You may also feel like you two can work through it and that "everything will be alright in the end." Women have a tendency to try to fix things with us men. It is a deep rooted *impression*. However, in this case there is nothing that you can fix. Standing by your man looks good in the movies and sounds good on a record, but the reality is that life with a man once incarcerated and now out is HARD! It will not be like it is in the movies. You will fix nothing with him, and life will be difficult. It will not be pretty, and there will not be a happy ending. Even if it works out, the road will be very rocky all the way. Remember that the divorce rate for first-time marriages in this country is 49%. This is for people who do not have incarceration issues. What effect do you think this dynamic will have on this relationship? Do you think it will make it better or worse?

A relationship with a man in prison is possible. However, it will be a tremendous test of perseverance, endurance, and humility. To succeed, the man should learn a skill or trade. The couple should receive counseling before the issues begin, so that they will be ready for them when they arrive. And finally, the woman should COMPLETELY abandon her "fix it" mentality with this man. Be encouraging to him for sure, but don't try to do everything. This man will have to be a man and deal with the consequences of his actions in the work world and with you.

Question 10:

> • **Why do some men at various income levels/status seek interracial relationships? Primarily with White and Asian females?**

Answer:

Income level has nothing to do with it. A poor Black man if he had the opportunity would at least experiment with a White or Asian woman. Interracial dating in the higher income brackets is more prevalent than in the lower ones because poorer Black men do not come into contact with these two ethnic groups much. If they did, you would see more of it across the income spectrum.

I think I am safe to say that we as Black men think that White and Asian women are docile compared with African-American women. I think we as Black men believe that both White and Asian women although independent, do not emphasize it and wear it like a badge of honor. They may make more money than men, but they do not make this an issue with men. White and Asian women do not have a problem allowing men to make decisions in the relationship. A White or Asian woman understands that she can still get what she wants from him by being womanly. She does not come to him in an overbearing way to get what she wants. She knows that each person has a role, and she allows him to be a man, and she is the woman no matter what. She does this willingly and without resentment.

These are the perceived differences. Now none of this may be true. This is my point of view. As Black men, we do not want to have an emotional tug of war (fight) to decide who is going to make the final decision in the relationship. It seems to me that the independent Black woman has something to "prove" to the world and especially to us, her Black man. The process of "proving" in a relationship is a lot of work. The back-and-forth tussle of who will make the decisions takes a lot of energy and creates emotional injury that can take a lifetime to heal. It is an emotional fight that gets old quickly. Who wants that? Life is short. With an Asian or White woman you don't have to worry about this tussle. You as the man will wear the pants. Case closed. Period. That's what I believe. Recall from earlier that men want to *feel* like men around their woman. The independent Black woman has no time to be concerned about how her man *feels*. She is busy handling her business. This woman is concerned about how "she" *feels,* whatever about him.

The Black man in the higher income bracket dates women outside of his race, because he will not have to emotionally fight with his woman about who will play which role in the relationship. It is not a question of income. Black men with lesser amounts of money would date outside the race as well if he was exposed to more ethnically divergent women. We don't want to fight with you. We want to be in a relationship with you.

Question 11:

- **I know that communication is needed for a strong relationship. But how can a couple communicate when only one person (the woman) knows how?**

Answer:

The answer to this question is for men as well as women. First, I will provide a brief psychological answer. Then, I will provide an in-depth practical one.

From a psychological point of view, men and women would be well served to keep in mind the definition of manhood in this society as the ability to provide for one's family. Additionally, there is the simultaneous belief in this same society that it is not "manly" to be emotional let alone show your emotions. Both of these mindsets create the dynamic that leads to the inability of men to communicate with women.

I have spoken in great detail about the *impression* left on men from the idea that we must provide for our families. However, what about the unconscious *impression* left on women from this same idea? A woman with a man who provides for her based upon this definition will be **<u>secure</u>**. This definition reinforces a mentality that women have in general across the color divide. Women want the protection of a man and the security he provides by ensuring that her actual needs will be met. (Food, shelter and clothing.) So women are left with the want/need and or desire for **security** from the same *impression*.

Now this is important. Based upon my research and conversations with the woman who participated in this work, it is apparent that **security** for a woman manifests in many different ways. Some women want a man who is real big and buff. Some women want a man who is very wealthy. Women differ, and the manifestation of how they want to feel their sense of **security** is not the same. However, there is one area that I submit ALL women derive a sense of **security** from— communication. Women derive a sense of **security** from talking. It does not matter what is being discussed. The answers to the questions posed in the conversation provide women with the ability to do what's necessary for their well-being. Recall that women as a whole are very good at handling their business. Therefore with the right information, (not information that makes them feel good or bad per se) they will make decisions that are in their best interests.

I will now jump into the practical aspect of the answer. We as men have been conditioned to not be emotional. It is an unfortunate aspect of this culture. According to the present societal view, a man is not a man if he shows emotion. I recall as a small boy thinking that when things got bad, you just suck it up and suppress your feelings whatever they were. From what I knew, this is what men did. Now this next point is very important so if you get nothing else from this book get this. Ladies, we as men equate communication with emotionality. For us talking about our feelings is no different than acting out on them. So we don't communicate well because deep down inside, we believe that communication is a code for being emotional and emotions are supposed to be suppressed. This is the underlying cause for our inability to communicate.

One thing we, as men, have never realized is that you, as women, equate communication with **security**. I believe this is the reason why women say they want us to be truthful and completely honest with them. Women communicate problems in a relationship for much more than the attempt to solve them. There is more going on within them than just getting a resolution. A woman *feels* **secure** when we engage in the communication process. From their perspective, this shows her that we really care. Interestingly it does not matter what the ultimate resolution is. The resolution could be positive or negative. Either resolution provides the woman with a sense of **security.** In a case where a decision is made to end the relationship, (a seemingly very bad thing) this woman will now know that it is time for her to move on and she will. The **security** of the communication allows her to shut off her "fix it" way of being. Without the communication, she will continue trying to do whatever she can to "fix" the problem. She can't help it, because that's all she knows how to do. Once she becomes **secure** in knowing where she stands (even if painful) she will now be able to move on.

We as men have not ever looked at the communication dynamic from the perspective that it provides **security** for you. We don't have a problem defending your honor or wanting to provide things for you to make you happy. I think that it is in our nature to want to provide **security** for you. It is a part of what makes a man a man according to the prevalent mindset of society today. When we begin to equate communication with **security** we will quickly communicate more. Unfortunately we as men "see" communication as "emotional." Therefore, we shun doing it. When we begin to see it as another means of providing **security** for our women, our mindset will change. We will see communication as a means of "being" a man and not the other way around. This would be a welcome change for all of us.

Question 12:

- **If you are a good woman and you cook, clean love and take care of your man, the home, the children, go to church, etc., why do men run from you?**

Answer:

The phrase in the question "good woman" is relative. "Good" to one person may not mean "good" to another. So the fact that "you" may think "you" are a "good" woman may or may not be true depending on the man you are dealing with at different points in time.

There is probably more going on that is having men run from this type of woman than meets the eye.

It is true that we as Black men love all the things listed above. Frankly, I would assert that men across the color divide love those things. We all want a woman who will cook, clean, love and take care of us, the home and the children. But we can get all these things from a maid or our mothers, except the loving part. And the loving part can be gotten elsewhere without strings attached. What else is being brought to the table? Do you want to wear the pants in the relationship? Do you insist on it? Do we get along? Not from the perspective of having fun. But from the perspective of *feeling* like you respect us?

For those of us who are not yet ready for a new "practice" in relationships, we have a need to *feel* like a man. The lack of fulfillment of this need will have men running.

Question 13

> • **You are a physically attractive woman, educated, independent, and religious above all—but you have needs—does a man look down on you if you sleep with him?**

Answer:

We as men don't look down on the women we sleep with unless we find that she is sleeping with everybody else. It's the educated, independent and religious part of the woman that may change our outlook on her.

An insecure male personality may find a high level of education and independence intimidating. Additionally, women with this education and independence may flaunt it. Generally speaking, the truth falls in the middle as men have insecure tendencies with these types of women, while women have egotistical tendencies based on their achievements.

One area where men have a big problem, is religion. I shudder at the thought of religious women. Not because I want to be with an ungodly woman or because I am an ungodly man. Religious women tend to want to convert us. They want us to go to church with them. Then they want us to join the church and get saved. If we choose **not** to do either, then we hear that you will pray for us. But why I am in need of prayer? If I have cancer you pray for me to help heal a disease of the body. But if there is nothing physically wrong with me are you praying for what you consider a mental disease on my part? It seems to me that you are praying for us because you think we are spiritually sick because we have not accepted your form of salvation. However, my lack of attendance at your church or my rejection of your means of deliverance does not make me ungodly. It just means that your way may not be the way for me.

If this is the reason for the prayers, then this means that you see me as lacking something based upon what YOU consider to be right. In my book this is just a subtle way of negatively being in judgment about me. This type of prayer I can do without.

So the push for us to adopt your religion will surely turn us off. Depending on the level of the push, it will give us a reason to look down on you and your actions especially when they are not in accordance with the religious teachings you espouse. A tit-for-tat judgment for judgment will start from you to me and back again. This is something that we can do without.

Question 14:

- **Is a woman over 45 unattractive to men her age?**

Answer:

Not hardly. Attraction to women over 45 has nothing to do with looks. Men over 45 have many options to choose from when deciding to date. Men at this age have probably been divorced once or twice. We are very set in our ways. (Just like women over 45) Often we do not want to compromise in a relationship. We prefer someone who likes us just the way we are. (who doesn't?) We know that an older woman will be just as set in her ways as we are in ours, therefore, a relationship with a woman over 45 will probably require more work since the both of us are equally set in our way of being. Everyone compromised in their younger days. Now, after reaching the age of 40 and above, neither men nor women want to alter their present way of being.

Older men do not have to deal with this set-way-of-being mentality with younger women. There are other things to deal with like immaturity, but we willingly trade this for what we get from them. Younger women look up to older men. It may or may not be true, but it seems like the younger woman has an automatic sense of respect for an older man. (This is not always the case with an older woman.) This respect is very important to us as we derive a certain sense of manhood from being looked up to by our women.

Younger women don't seem to throw out the "I don't need a man" comments with the same fervor and pitch as older women. Although it may be just as true, I think that younger women are more accepting of the help or means of providing that we give them. So even though younger women may also use the "I don't need a man" term, their application of it to an older man seems to me to be quite different.

Everyone "practicing" relationships from the current societal view is involved in them for the satisfaction of a want/need and or desire. Older men desire younger women because we believe that they provide the best means of satisfying our wants/needs.

This may or may not be true. If we believed that an older woman would best satisfy them, we would date her instead. It is a continuation of the "what-have-you-done-for-me-lately mentality" present in most relationships today.

Question 15:

 • **Why are Black men living under a slavery mentality?**

Answer:

Because the mentality of slavery never really changed. Although the institution of slavery ended more than a hundred years ago, the "mind-set" of slavery did not. Even today you hear people in the African-American community use the term, "this is a white man's world". However, a review of history prior to two thousand years ago and to the beginning of the first life on Earth shows that this is anything but true.

But why would truth matter if you do not believe the truth? One of the unfortunate effects from the institution of slavery was the "belief" and then "ratification" of certain ideas in both the African-American and European communities. Europeans (whites) began to believe the "idea" that they were superior to the African-American. (and to all other ethnic groups as well) Conversely, the African-American began to believe the "idea" that they were inferior to Europeans.

There is nothing "true" about the superiority or inferiority of one group over another. The truth is that ALL people are the same inside and out except for the outer "appearance" which differs in the amount of melanin in a person's skin. However, the skin of a person is an organ so the difference in color of one group to another is just that, an "appearance" based upon a way of "seeing" people from their differences as opposed to their similarities.

The belief in the superior and inferior "ideas" of both the African-American and European created unconscious *impressions* which still exist presently. As *unconscious impressions* drive the personality of a person unknowingly (unconsciously), recognizing them is very difficult. Generally speaking, a person being "driven" by an *unconscious impression* would not know they were being "driven". All they would know is that they "felt" a particular way. So the term used earlier, "this is a white man's world", would be said by a person because of the idea "that's just the way I am" and because that's "how I feel".

So Black men have a slave mentality because the mentality of slavery did not end when the institution of slavery did. The mentality continued on. However, the slave mentality is not confined to a mental belief of inferiority vs. superiority. It is much more than that and goes deeper. The mentality is a way of thinking. But the mentality of slavery does not solely reside in the mind of

African-American men. It also resides in other ethnic groups and with women as well.

I believe that no person can be physically enslaved by another unless he or she is first mentally a slave to themselves. A person who is not "free" mentally is a person who is not in control of themselves or their emotions. Very few people live life free of the hold of their emotions. In fact, it is apparent that people as a whole are slaves to emotions. For example, when the emotion of anger presents itself, without thought, we yell or lash out. When the emotion of happiness presents itself, without thought, we smile and feel good. When the emotion of sadness presents itself, without thought, we get sullen or withdraw or cry. For most of us, as soon as the emotion pops up, we immediately respond (jump) to it. This process is no different than the slave on the plantation "jumping" when the slave master said "jump".

My definition of slavery is having a mindset that limits our ability to think for ourselves and substitutes that with a way of thinking based on instinct instead. It is my belief that people in general and across ethnic groupings are slaves to themselves. (i.e., emotions)

This should not be surprising in a culture where the overriding way of life is to eat, drink and be merry. This mindset is a mindset predicated on acting on emotion(s). So the mindset itself encourages a slave mentality. Not to a specific person or thing, but to our ability to think clearly and free from our emotions. Carter G. Woodson in his book, *The Mis-Education of the*

Negro, said very eloquently that shackles are not needed to enslave a person: "Teach him that his place of entering an establishment is in the back of the place and soon he will go there automatically". Today no one has to be told to act based upon emotion yet the prevalent mentality is to do just that.

So it is not just Black men who presently live under a slave mentality. Anyone who immediately acts based upon emotion without thought or reflection (where there is no exercise of choice) is living under a slave mentality.

So my answer to the question is why wouldn't Black men live under a slave mentality? We are no different than anyone else!

A NOTE ABOUT THE AUTHOR

LAWRENCE R. MATHEWS (ANPU WASET) WAS BORN AND RAISED IN DETROIT, MICHIGAN. HE IS THE FIRST IN HIS IMMEDIATE FAMILY TO GRADUATE FROM COLLEGE, COMPLETING HIS STUDIES AT WESTERN MICHIGAN UNIVERSITY IN 1986. HE RECEIVED A BACHELOR OF BUSINESS ADMINISTRATION, B.B.A. DEGREE. HE IS ALSO THE FIRST TO ATTEND GRADUATE SCHOOL, COMPLETING HIS STUDIES AT MICHIGAN STATE UNIVERSITY DETROIT COLLEGE OF LAW IN 1996. HE RECEIVED A JURIS DOCTOR, J.D. DEGREE.

MR. MATHEWS WORKED AS AN EDUCATOR FOR THE DETROIT PUBLIC SCHOOLS FOR APPROXIMATELY EIGHT YEARS AND AS AN ATTORNEY FOR NINE YEARS. HE HAS PRACTICED BEFORE THE MICHIGAN SUPREME COURT, THE MICHIGAN COURT OF APPEALS, AND HAS HAD MORE THAN 25 JURY TRIALS MAINLY AS A CIVIL DEFENSE ATTORNEY.

MR. MATHEWS IS DIVORCED. HE IS THE FATHER OF TWO DAUGHTERS KHADEEJA AND NAILAH, AND IS THE GRANDFATHER OF ELIJAH.

MR. MATHEWS IS THE AUTHOR OF THE BOOK **"YOU! ARE RESPONSIBLE FOR YOUR LIFE!"** HE ALSO WRITES A MONTHLY COLUMN FOR THE MAGAZINE **"IN THE BLACK"** CALLED **"A BETTER WAY."** THE MAGAZINE IS PUBLISHED BY THE ARIZONA BLACK PAGES. HE IS ALSO THE CREATOR OF THE **"INSPIRATIONAL PHILOSOPHY"** LECTURE SERIES. "INSPIRATIONAL PHILOSOPHY" IS THE STUDY OF ANCIENT PHILOSOPHICAL SYSTEMS WHICH ARE THEN APPLIED TO COMMON SITUATIONS OF TODAY IN AN INSPIRATIONAL WAY.

"A Black Man, My Point of View"

His other interests include the practice of yoga, meditation, and vegetarianism. He studies ancient philosophies and religions. He is currently a practioner of Egyptian Yoga and a student and practicing yogi at the Sema Institute and University of Yoga in Miami, Florida.